PIANO • VOCAL • GUITAR

BEST OF
Donna Summer

ISBN 978-1-5400-3133-4

Visit Hal Leonard Online at
www.halleonard.com

Contact us:
Hal Leonard
7777 West Bluemound Road
Milwaukee, WI 53213
Email: info@halleonard.com

In Europe, contact:
Hal Leonard Europe Limited
42 Wigmore Street
Marylebone, London, W1U 2RN
Email: info@halleonardeurope.com

In Australia, contact:
Hal Leonard Australia Pty. Ltd.
4 Lentara Court
Cheltenham, Victoria, 3192 Australia
Email: info@halleonard.com.au

Donna Summer

LaDonna Adrian Gaines. Donna Gaines. Gayn Pierre. Donna Sommer. Regardless of what one calls her, one fact remains: Donna Summer was the undisputed Queen of Disco. Her prominence on the dance charts of the disco era made her both a cultural icon and one of the defining pop-music voices of the time, influencing later singers as disparate as Madonna and Beyoncé. And unlike other disco stars whose luminance waned as the music itself became less popular in the 1980s, Donna had the talent and determination to move past the genre and segue into a pop-rock sound.

Born in Boston on December 31, 1948, Donna left for New York City just weeks prior to her high school graduation. After a blues-rock band gig fell through, she auditioned for the musical *Hair*, landing the part of Sheila in the Munich, Germany production of the show. She soon became fluent in German, and within three years had moved to Vienna, Austria, where she joined the Vienna Folk Opera. In 1973, she married Austrian actor Helmuth Sommer. From the Anglicization of his last name, she became Donna Summer.

In Munich, she was destined to meet local writer and producer Giorgio Moroder and his songsmith partner Pete Bellotte. With them, Summer recorded the 1974 album *Lady of the Night*. The next year, she pitched "Love to Love You Baby" to them. Moroder soon transformed the song into the 17-minute sexually charged track that became a clubland hit. A couple of years later, the hit single "I Feel Love" made a huge impact; its trance-like dance electronica was a totally new sound for a pop song, and its dichotomy of the human voice against a completely synthetic accompaniment subsequently echoed through innumerable club hits.

Donna's cover of "MacArthur Park" (1978) scored her first chart-topping single, a triumph she repeated with "Hot Stuff," "Bad Girls," and "No More Tears (Enough Is Enough)" — the latter a duet with the legendary Barbra Streisand. "Last Dance," a song that has ended many a wedding reception — taken from the soundtrack of *Thank God It's Friday* (1978), her film-acting debut — won Summer her first Grammy and garnered an Academy Award for Best Song. "Hot Stuff" scored another Grammy for her.

Across her career, Donna went on to pile up 14 Top 10 singles in the United States, winning five Grammy Awards. Producer-songwriter David Foster said she "changed the face of pop music forever," and spoke of her "class, dignity, and grace." In a 2003 interview, the Queen of Disco herself opined, "This music will always be with us. I mean, whether they call it disco music or hip-hop or bebop or flip-flop, whatever they're going to call it, I think music to dance to will always be with us."

Following a protracted battle with lung cancer — ironically, she never smoked — Donna Summer died on May 17, 2012 at her home in Naples, Florida. She was 63 years old.

4   BAD GIRLS

12   DIM ALL THE LIGHTS

28   HEAVEN KNOWS

32   HOT STUFF

36   I FEEL LOVE

42   LAST DANCE

48   LOVE TO LOVE YOU BABY

54   MACARTHUR PARK

64   NO MORE TEARS (ENOUGH IS ENOUGH)

21   ON THE RADIO

76   SHE WORKS HARD FOR THE MONEY

82   STAMP YOUR FEET

90   STATE OF INDEPENDENCE

100   THIS TIME I KNOW IT'S FOR REAL

105   UNCONDITIONAL LOVE

112   THE WANDERER

BAD GIRLS

Words and Music by DONNA SUMMER,
JOE "BEANS" ESPOSITO, EDDIE HOKENSON
and BRUCE SUDANO

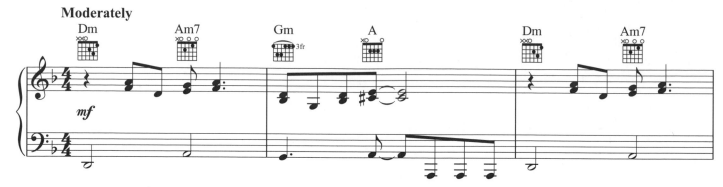

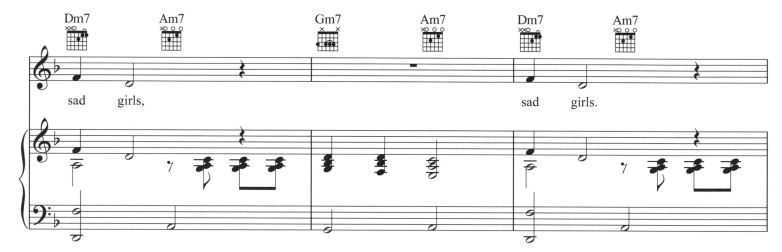

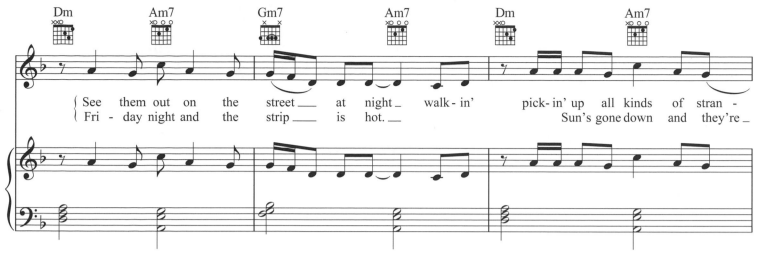

See them out on the street _ at night _ walk-in' pick-in' up all kinds of stran-
Fri-day night and the strip _ is hot. _ Sun's gone down and they're _

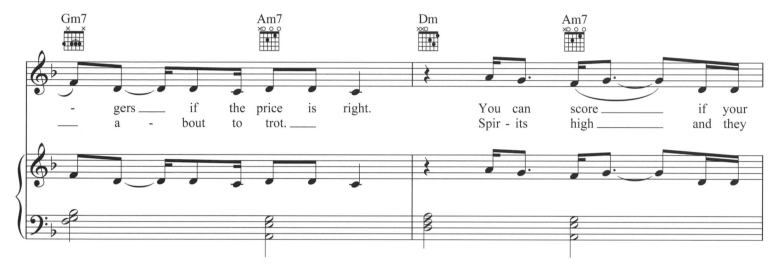

-gers _ if the price is right. You can score _ if your
_ a-bout to trot. _ Spir-its high _ and they

pock-et's nice. _ But you want a good time. _
look so hot. _ Do you want to get down? _

You ask your-self _
Now don't you ask your-self _

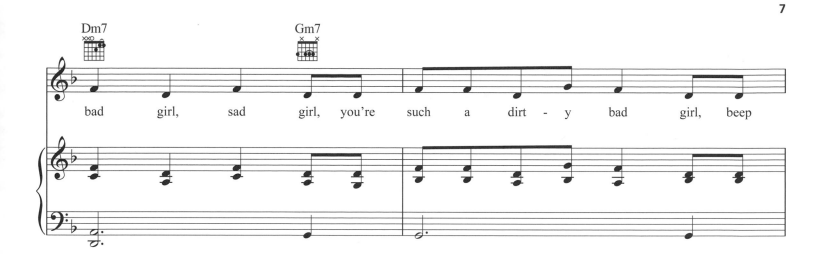

bad girl, sad girl, you're such a dirt - y bad girl, beep

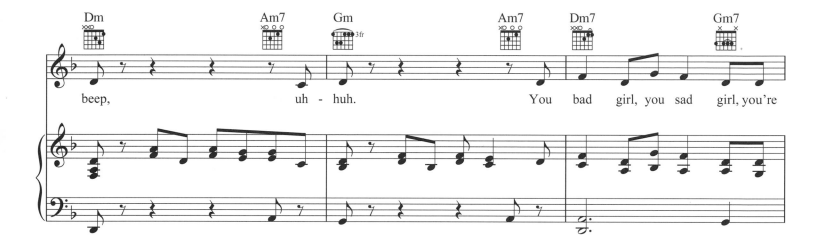

beep, uh - huh. You bad girl, you sad girl, you're

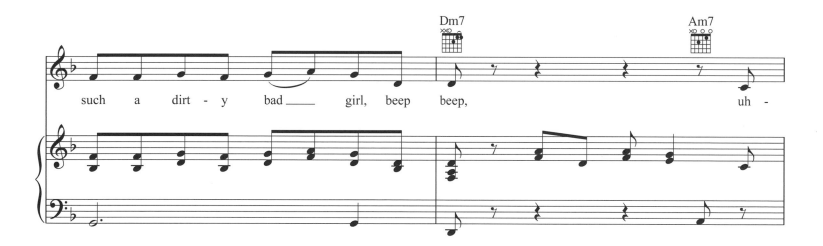

such a dirt - y bad ___ girl, beep beep, uh -

huh. Now you and me we're both ___ the same, ___

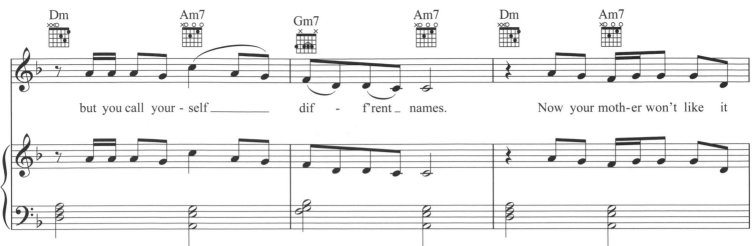

but you call your - self _____ dif - f'rent _ names. Now your moth-er won't like it

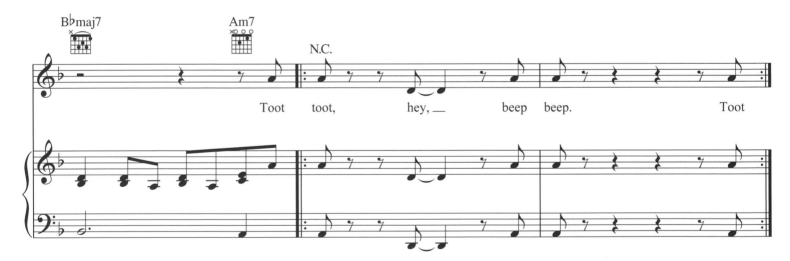

when she finds out ___ the girl is out at night.

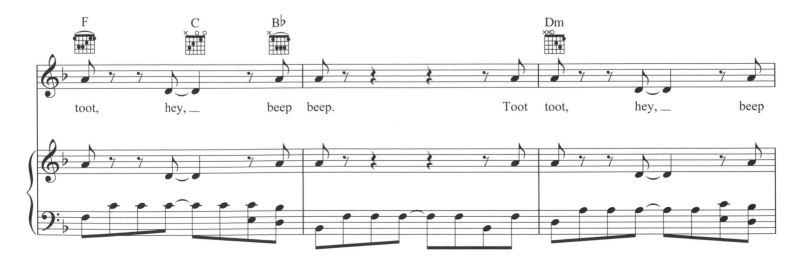

Toot toot, hey, ___ beep beep. Toot

toot, hey, ___ beep beep. Toot toot, hey, ___ beep

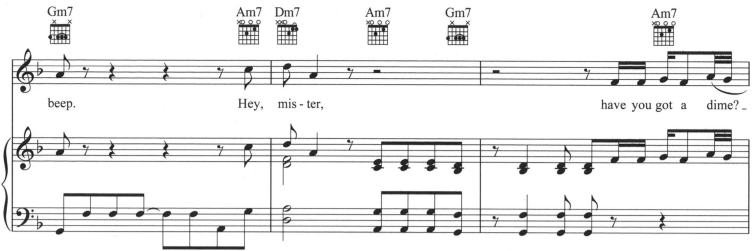

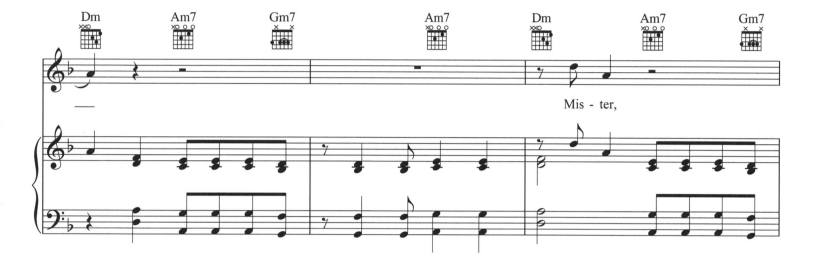

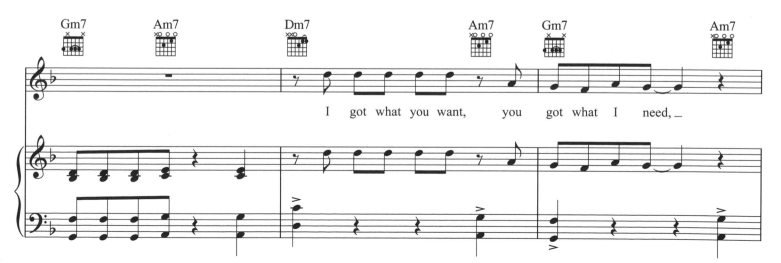

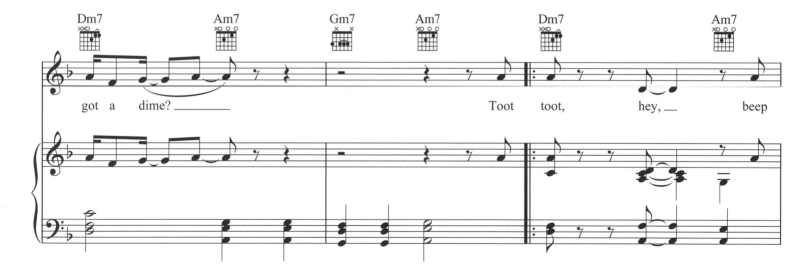

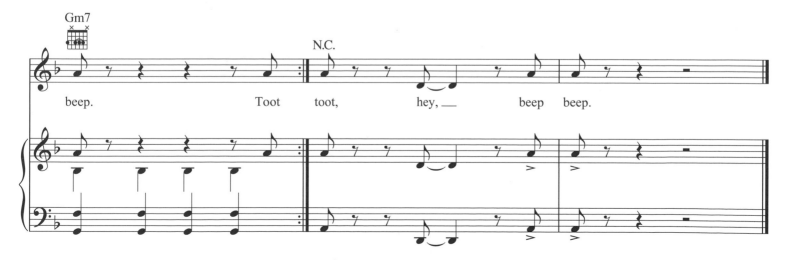

DIM ALL THE LIGHTS

Words and Music by
DONNA SUMMER

Moderate Ballad

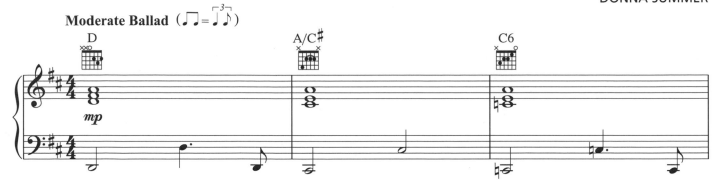

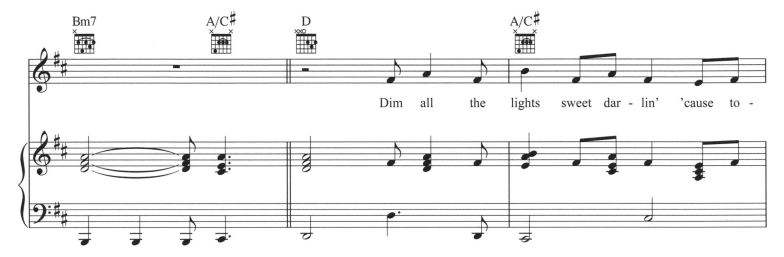

Dim all the lights sweet dar-lin' 'cause to-

night it's all ____ the way. ____ Turn up the

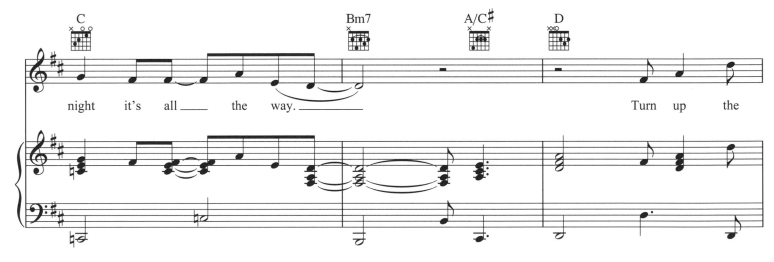

old Vic-tro-la, gon-na dance the night ____ a-way. ____

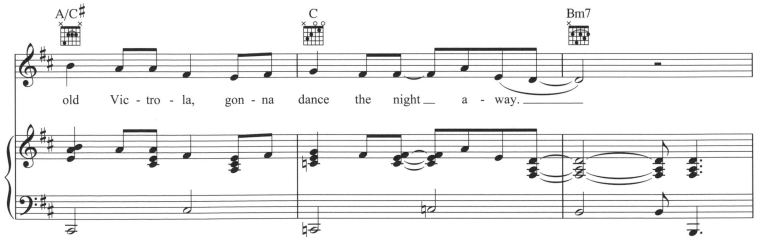

13

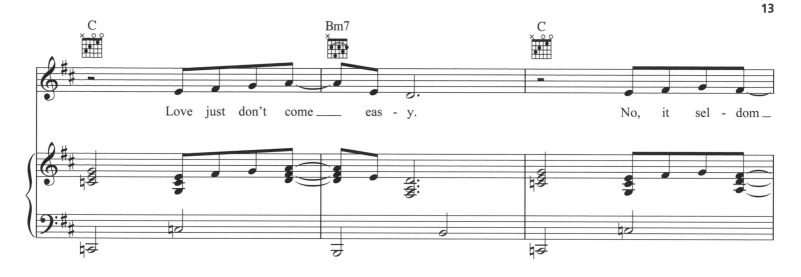

Love just don't come ___ eas - y. No, it sel - dom ___

___ does. ___ When you find ___ the per - fect love, ___

Disco, straight eighths

let it fill ___ you up. ___

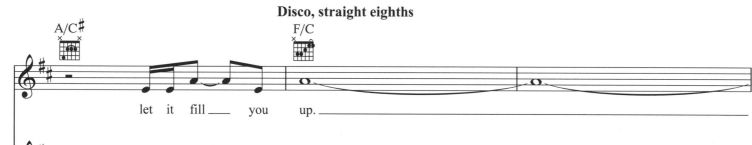

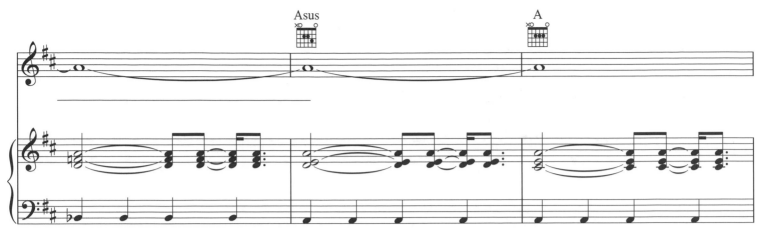

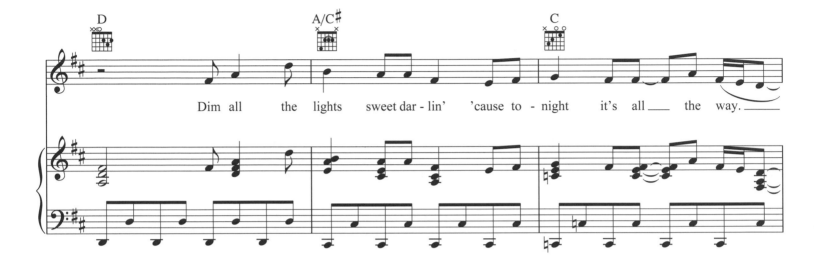

Dim all the lights sweet dar-lin' 'cause to-night it's all ___ the way. ___

Hey ___ ba - by, turn up the old Vic-tro-la, gon-na

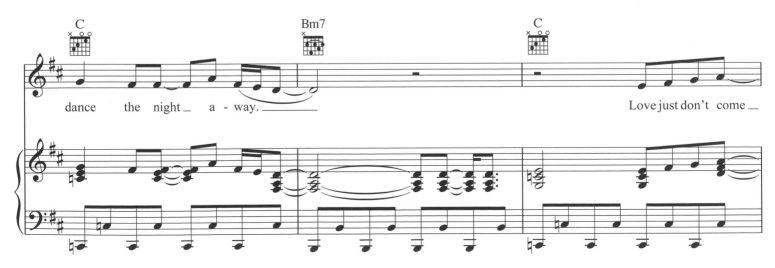

dance the night ___ a - way. ___   Love just don't come ___

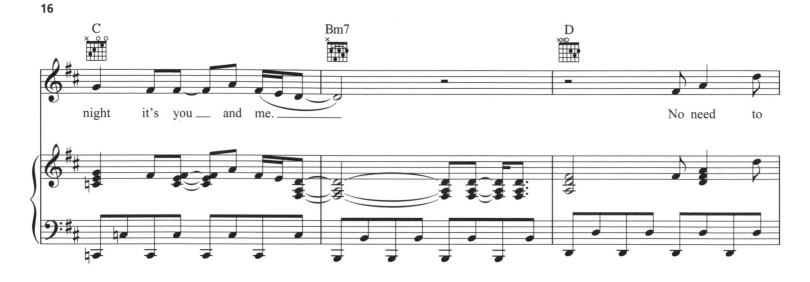

night it's you ___ and me. ____ No need to

wor - ry, dar - lin', 'cause we're all we real - ly need. ____

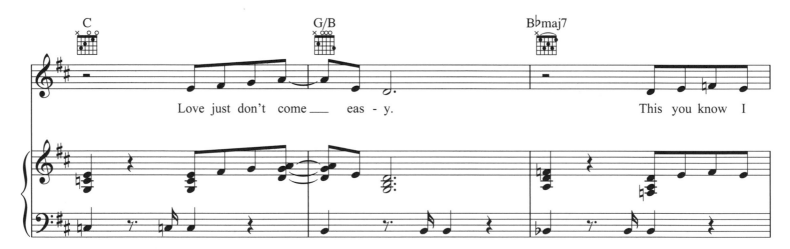

Love just don't come ___ eas - y. This you know I

un - der - stand. ____ Want to be your ___ wom - an. ____

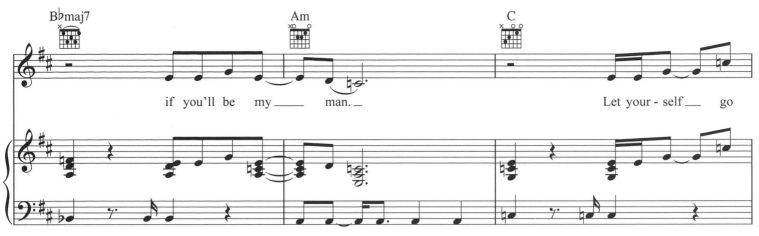

if you'll be my ____ man. ____ Let your - self ____ go

free - ly ____ and I'll ____ show you things ____ that you've dreamed of. ____

Don't think that you're dream - in', ____ we've found the

per - fect love. We've found the per - fect love ____ and I'm like a cup, ____ come

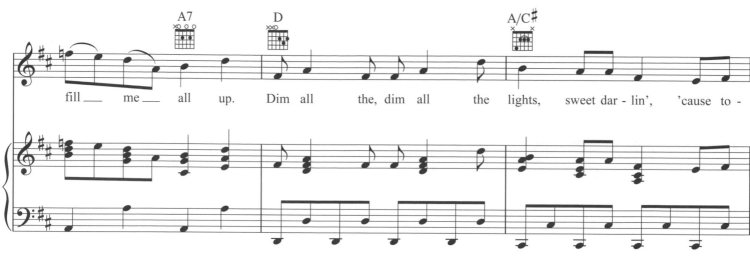

fill___ me___ all up. Dim all the, dim all the lights, sweet dar-lin', 'cause to-

night it's all___ the way. ___ Whoa ba - by, turn up the

old Vic - tro - la, gon - na dance the night___ a - way. ___

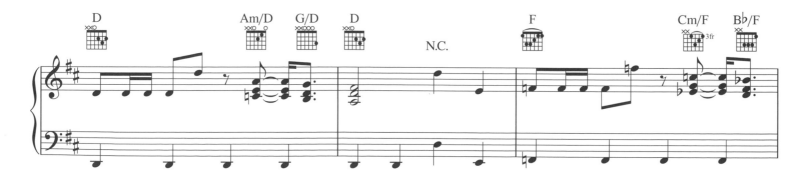

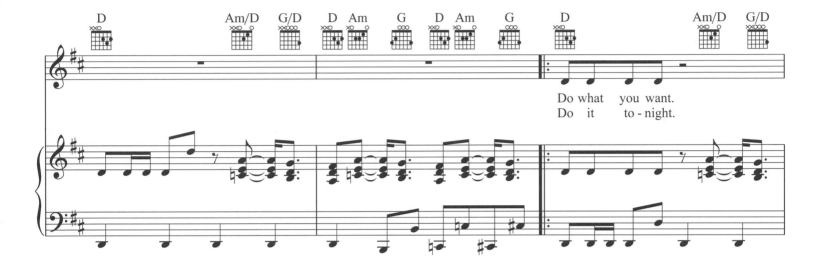

Do what you want.
Do it to - night.

You can use me all up. Take me
You know the mo-ment's so right. Turn my

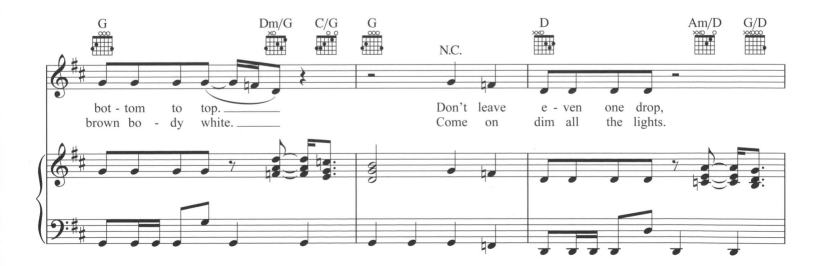

bot - tom to top. Don't leave e - ven one drop,
brown bo - dy white. Come on dim all the lights.

no. ___ no, no, no, no, no.

D   **A/C#**   **C**

Dim all the, dim all the lights, sweet dar-lin', 'cause to-night it's all___ the way. ___
(Lead vocal ad lib on repeat and fade.)

Bm7   **D**   **A/C#**

___ Whoa,__ ba - by, turn up the old Vic-tro-la, gon-na

C   **Bm7**

dance the night__ a-way. ___

Repeat and Fade

Optional Ending
D

ON THE RADIO

Words and Music by DONNA SUMMER
and GIORGIO MORODER

Some-one found a let - ter you wrote __ me on the ra - di - o, __
Send - in' in a let - ter to tell __ them that I love you, too; __

and they told the world __ just how __ you felt. _____ It
if you hear it, may - be you __ will know. _____ When you

must have fall - en out of a hole in your old brown o - ver - coat; __ they
hear them read the line a - bout love's re - turn __ on the ra - di - o, __ you'll

said it real-ly loud, they said __ it on the air on the }
heard it real-ly loud, they said __ it on the air on the } ra-di - o,   Whoa _____

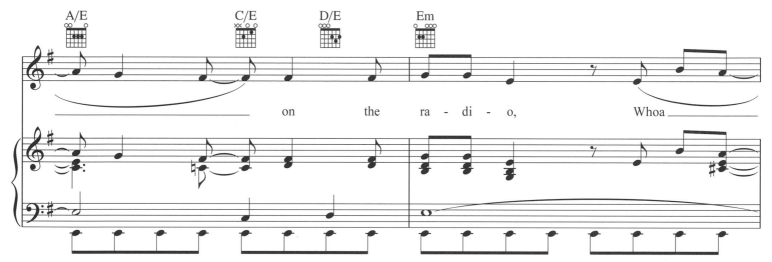

_____ on the ra - di - o,   Whoa _____

_____ on the ra - di - o,   Whoa _____ on the

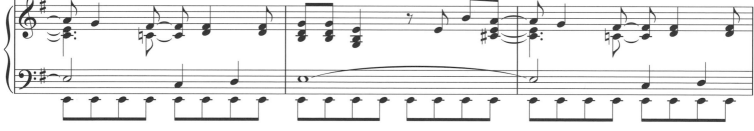

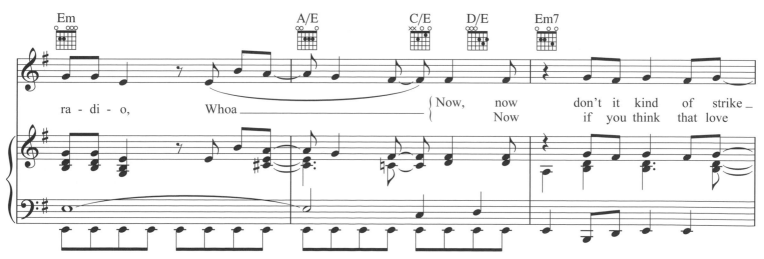

ra-di - o,   Whoa _____ { Now, now   don't it kind of strike __
                                    { Now   if you think   that love

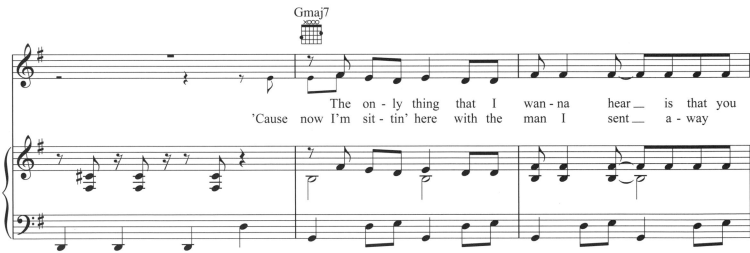

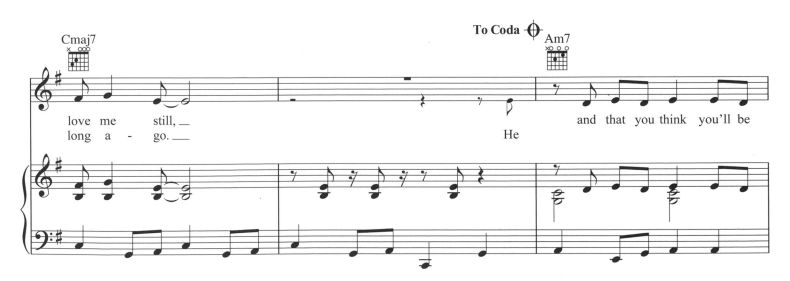

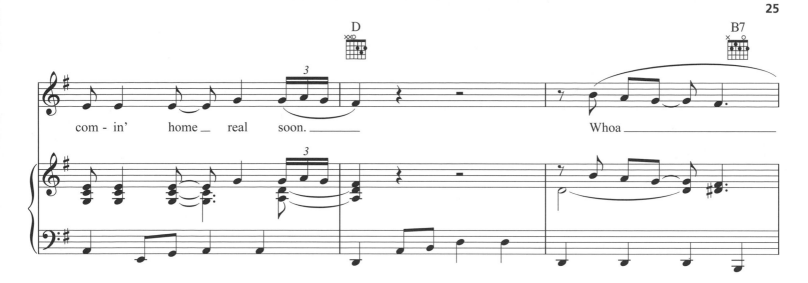

com - in' home _ real soon. _____ Whoa _____

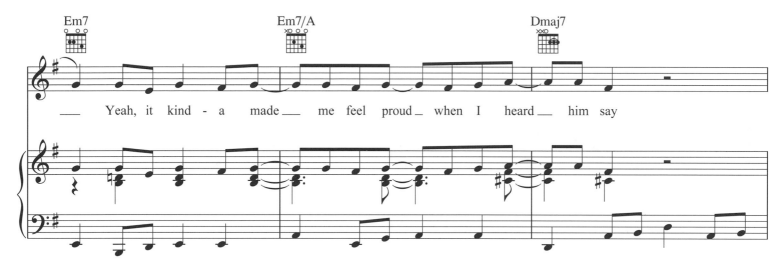

_ Yeah, it kind - a made _ me feel proud _ when I heard _ him say

you could - n't find the words _ to say _ it your - self. _

And now in my heart _ I know _

I can say ___ what I real-ly feel ___ 'cause they

said it real-ly loud, they said ___ it on the air, on the ra-di-o. Whoa ___

___ on the ra-di-o, Whoa ___ on the

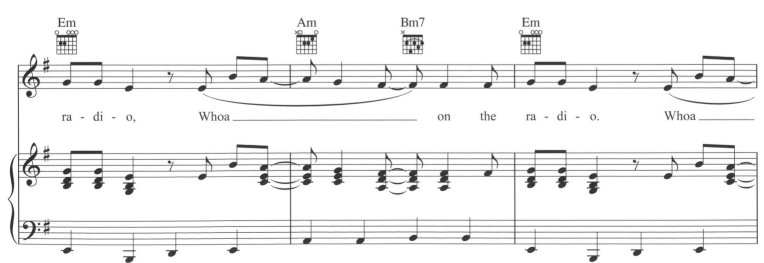

ra-di-o, Whoa ___ on the ra-di-o. Whoa ___

on the ra - di - o.

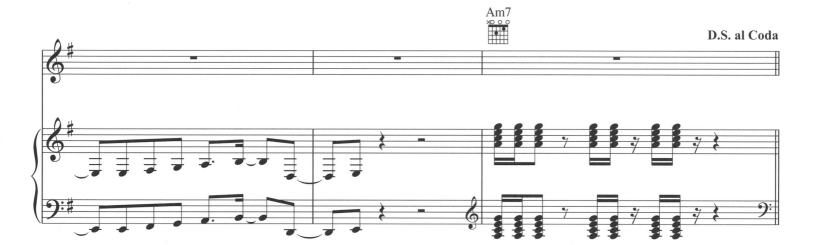

D.S. al Coda

CODA

fi - n'lly re - al - ized, he said___ it real - ly loud on the ra - di - o, whoa___

Repeat and Fade

_____ on the ra - di - o, whoa _____ on the

HEAVEN KNOWS

Words and Music by DONNA SUMMER,
GIORGIO MORODER, PETE BELLOTTE
and GREG MATTHIESON

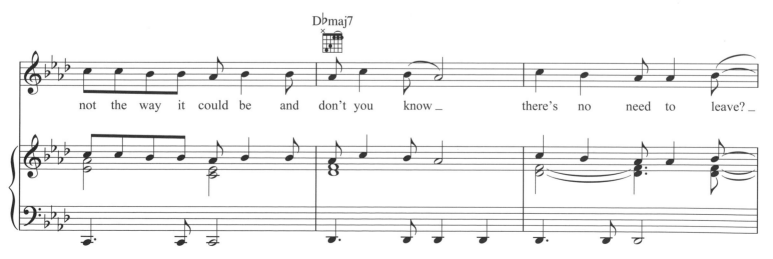

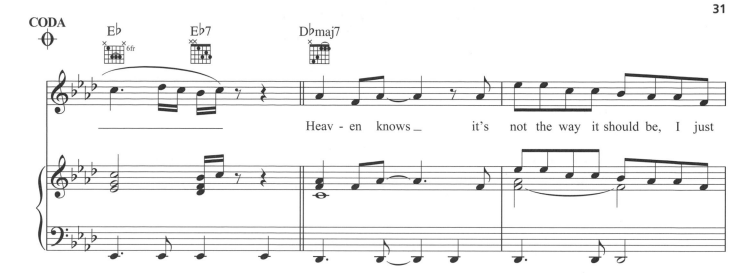

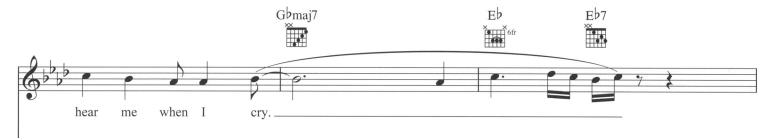

HOT STUFF

Words and Music by PETE BELLOTTE,
HAROLD FALTERMEIER and KEITH FORSEY

Moderate Disco

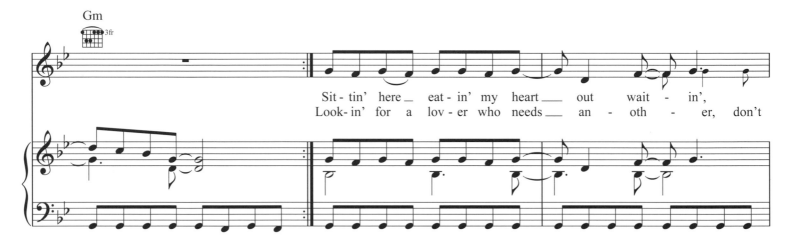

Sit - tin' here __ eat - in' my heart __ out wait - in',
Look - in' for a lov - er who needs __ an - oth - er, don't

wait - in' for some lov - er to call. __
want an - oth - er night on my own. __

Dialed a - bout a thou - sand num-
Wan - na share my love with a warm-

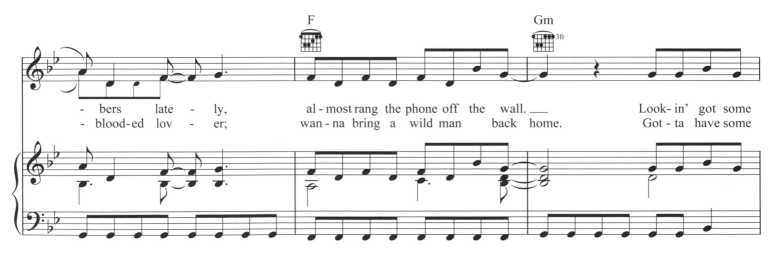

- bers late - ly,
- blood - ed lov - er;

al - most rang the phone off the wall. __
wan - na bring a wild man back home.

Look - in' got some
Got - ta have some

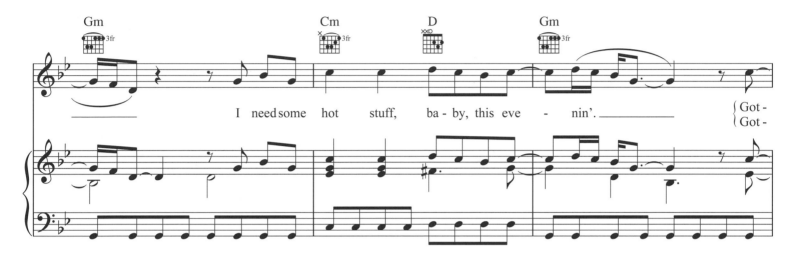

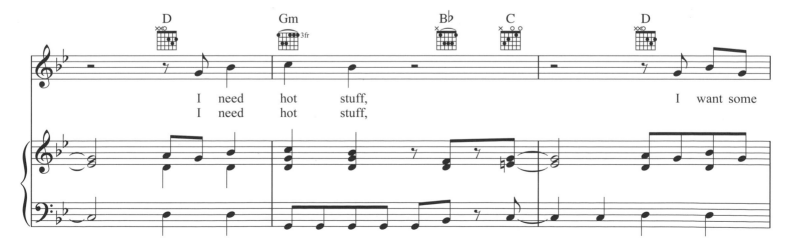

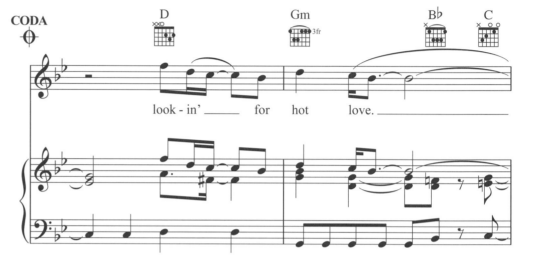

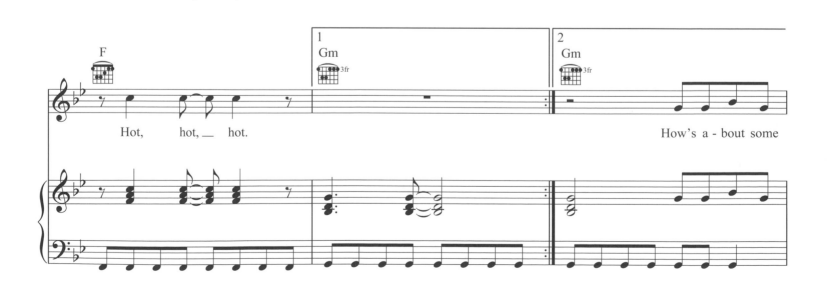

hot stuff, ba-by, this eve - nin'; ___ I need some hot stuff, ba-by, to - night. _

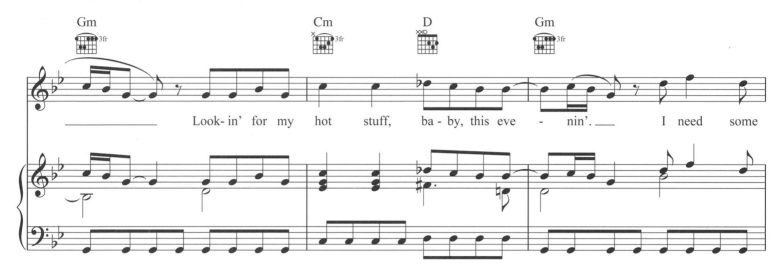

_____ Look-in' for my hot stuff, ba-by, this eve - nin'. ___ I need some

hot stuff, ba-by, to - night. __ Yeah, yeah, I want some hot stuff, ba-by, this eve -

Repeat and Fade

- nin'. ___ I want some hot stuff, ba-by, to - night. __ Yeah, yeah, yeah, yeah, now,

I FEEL LOVE

Words and Music by DONNA SUMMER,
GIORGIO MORODER and PETE BELLOTTE

Moderately fast

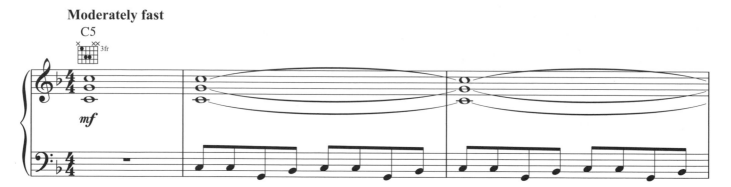

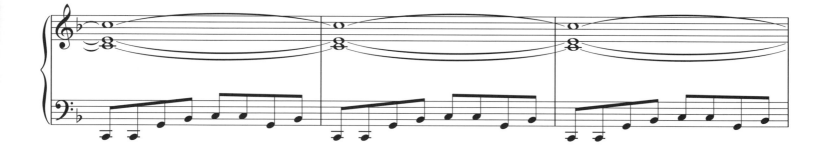

Ooh, _____

_____ it's so good, _ it's so good, _ it's so good, _ it's so good, _ it's so _____

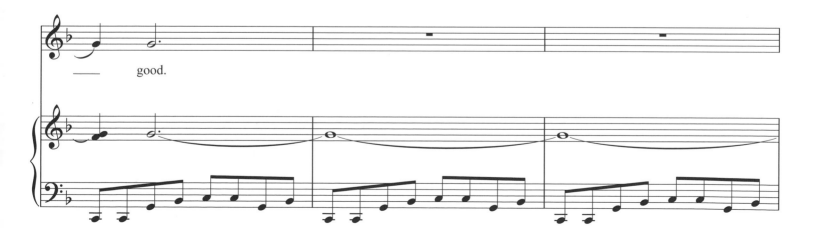

_____ good.

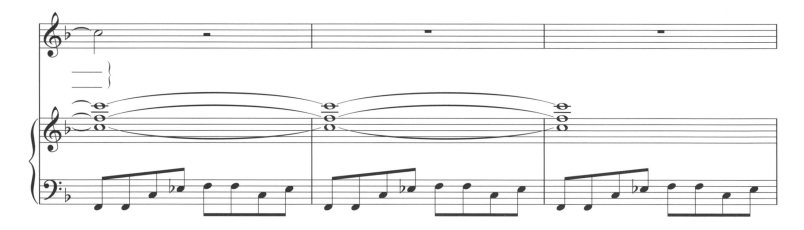

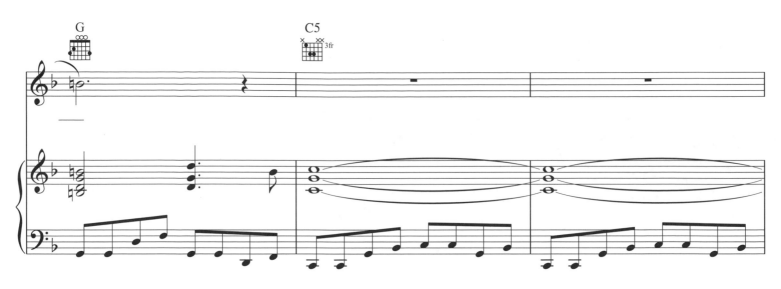

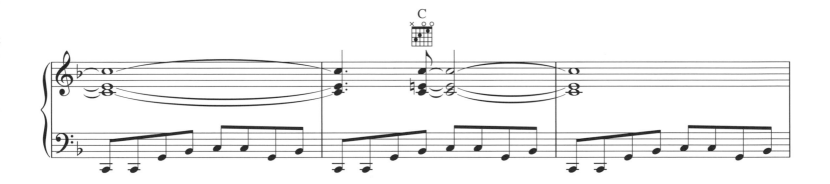

Ooh, _____ fall-ing free, __ fall-ing free, __ fall-ing free, __

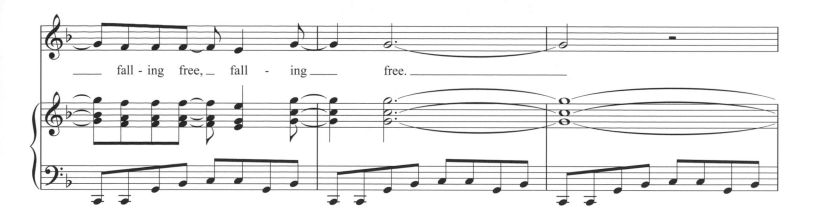

fall - ing free, __ fall - ing ____ free. _____

D.S. al Coda

CODA

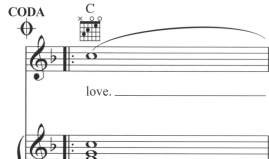

love. _____

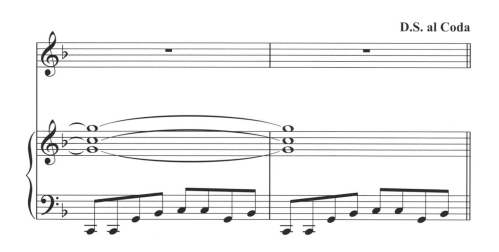

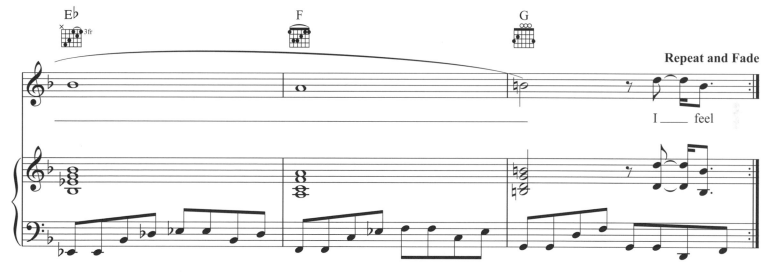

Repeat and Fade

_____ I ___ feel

Optional Ending

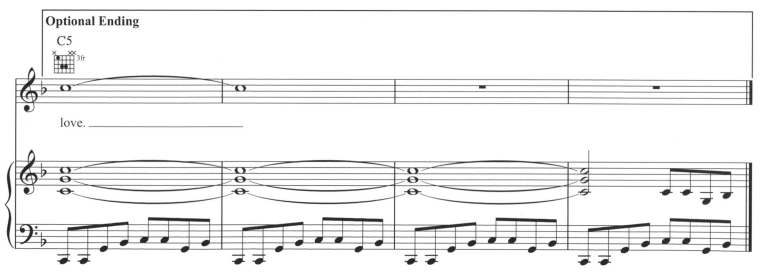

love. _____

LAST DANCE

Words and Music by
PAUL JABARA

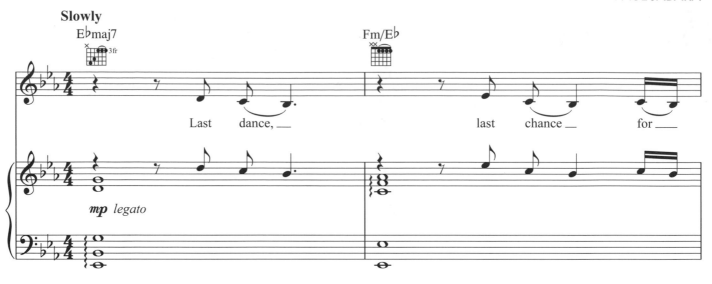

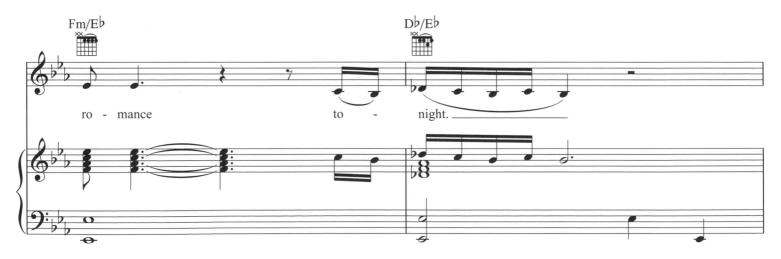

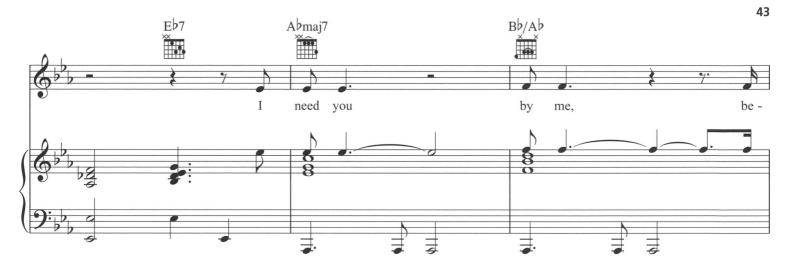

I need you by me, be-

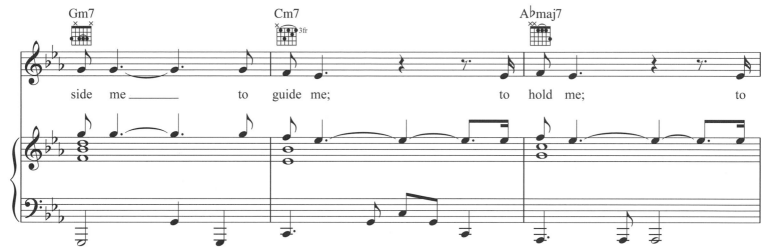

side me _____ to guide me; to hold me; to

scold me, 'cause when I'm bad, I'm so, so bad. _____

Medium Disco beat

So let's dance _____ the last dance, _____

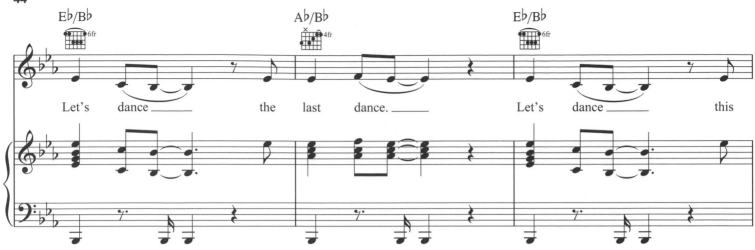

Let's dance ____ the last dance. ____ Let's dance ____ this

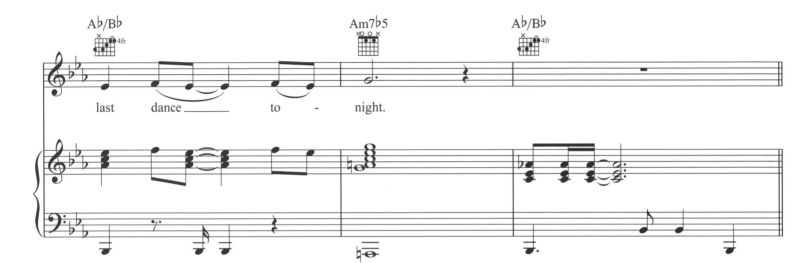

last dance ____ to - night.

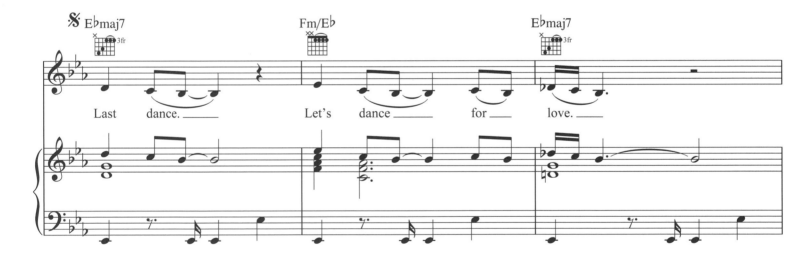

Last dance. ____ Let's dance ____ for ____ love. ____

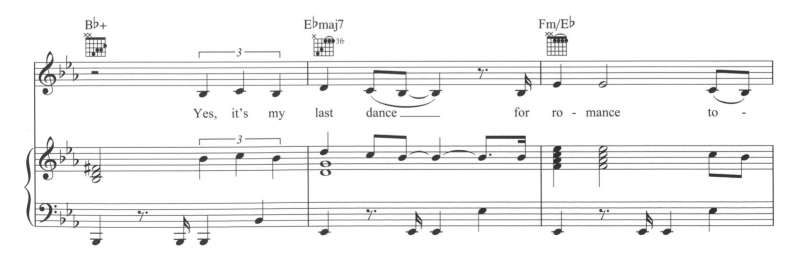

Yes, it's my last dance ____ for ro - mance to -

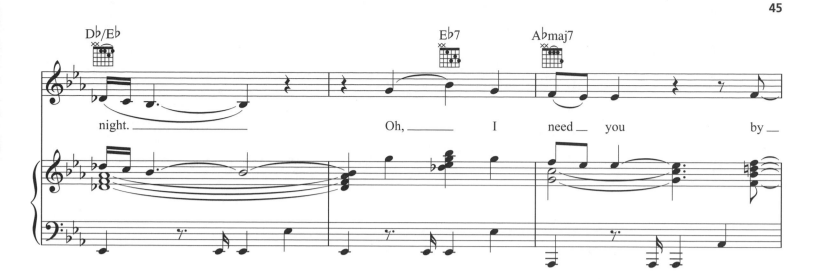

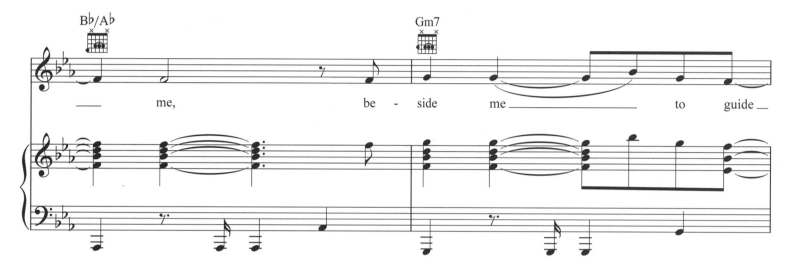

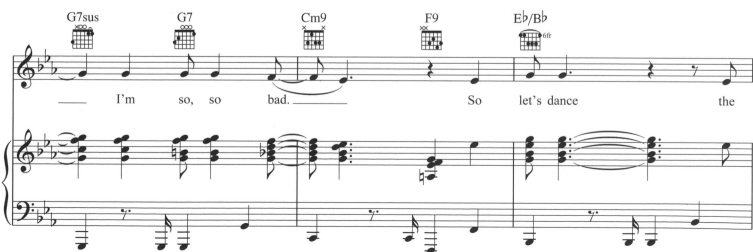

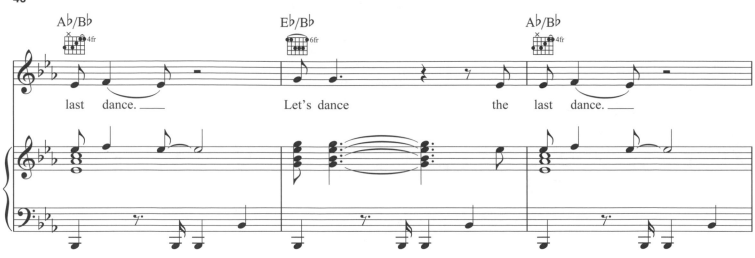

last dance. ____ Let's dance the last dance. ____

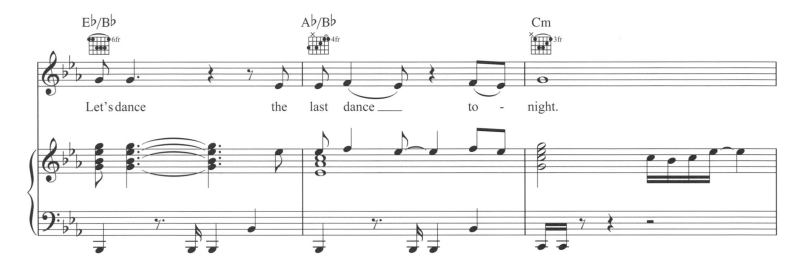

Let's dance the last dance ____ to - night.

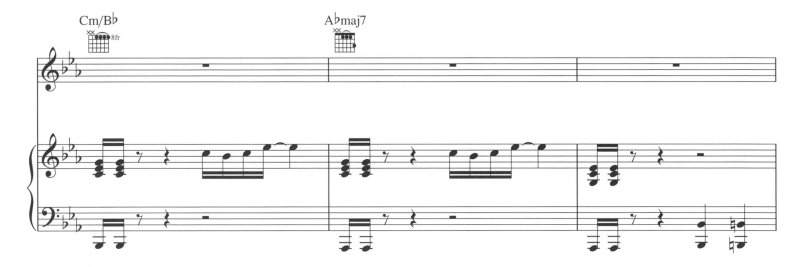

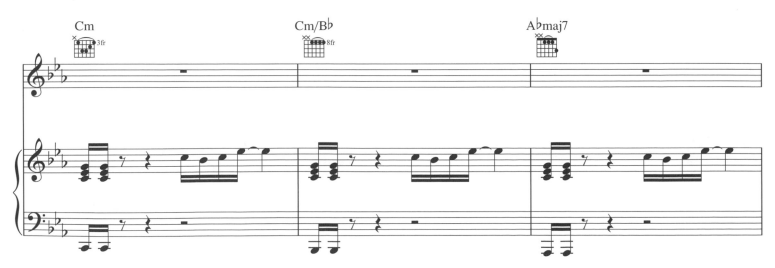

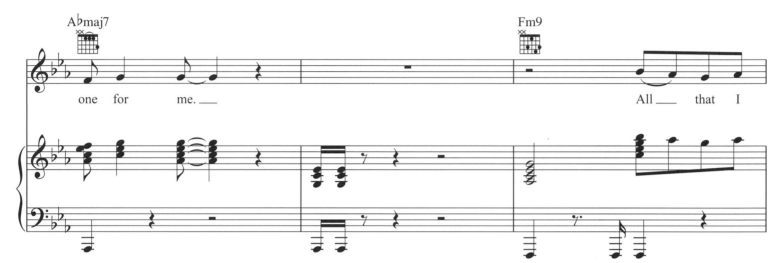

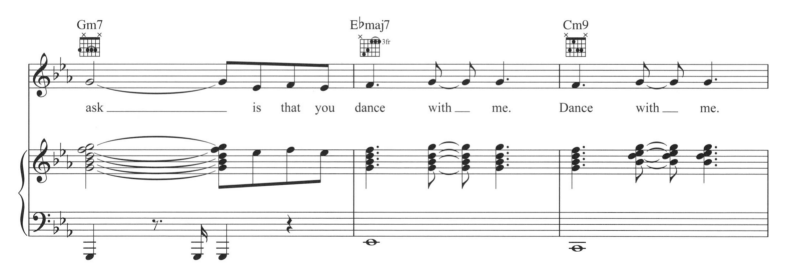

LOVE TO LOVE YOU BABY

Words and Music by DONNA SUMMER,
GIORGIO MORODER and PETE BELLOTTE

Moderate Disco

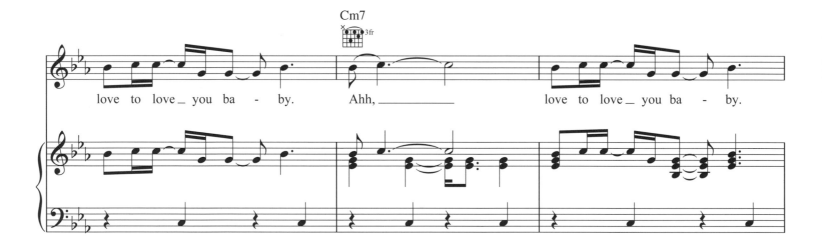

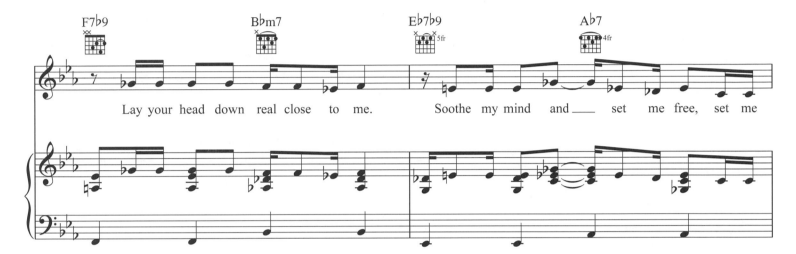

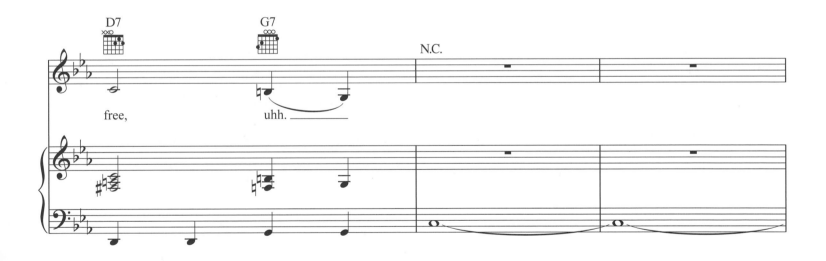

love to love _ you ba - by. Ahh, love to love _ you ba - by.

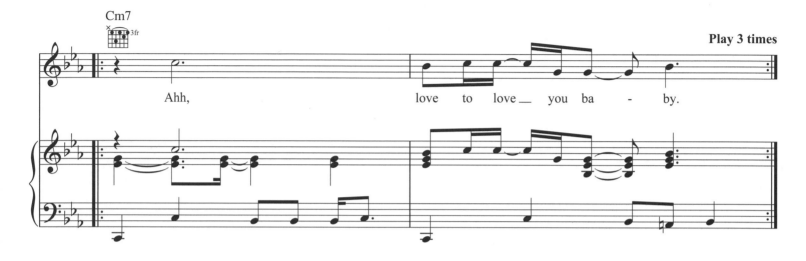

Play 3 times

Ahh, love to love _ you ba - by.

When you're lay-in' so _ close to me, there's no place I'd rath - er you be than with _

Play 3 times

_ me, uhh. _ Ahh, love to love _ you babe.

53

Do it to me a-gain___ and a-gain. You put me in such an___ aw-ful spin, in a

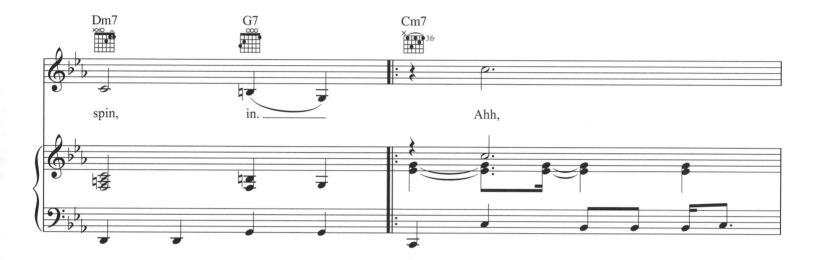

spin, in.___ Ahh,

love to love___ you babe.___ Ahh,

Optional Ending

Repeat and Fade

love to love___ you babe.___

MACARTHUR PARK

Words and Music by
JIMMY WEBB

Slowly, with feeling

Spring was nev-er wait-ing ___ for us

dear, it ran one ___ step a-head as we fol-lowed in ___ the dance.

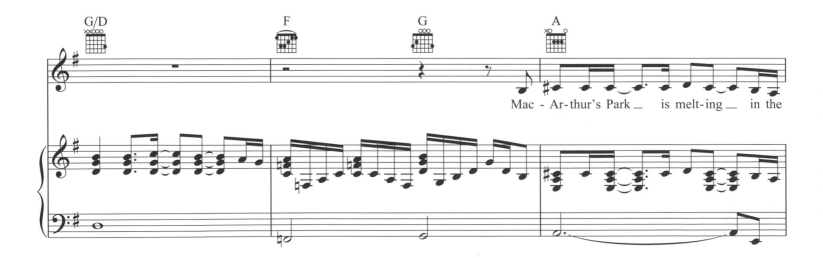

Mac-Ar-thur's Park ___ is melt-ing ___ in the

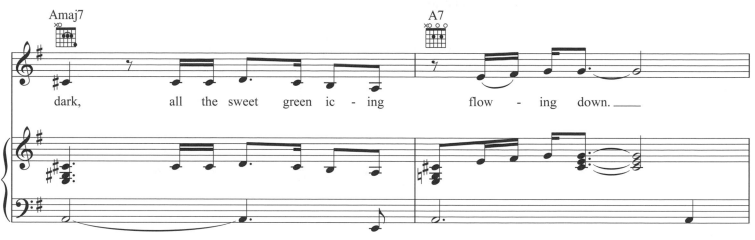

dark, all the sweet green ic - ing flow - ing down. ____

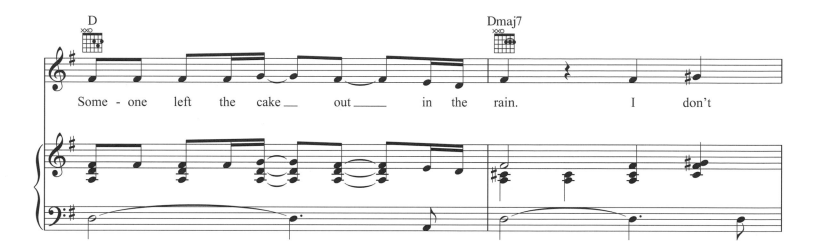

Some - one left the cake ____ out ____ in the rain. I don't

think that I ____ can take ____ it 'cause it took so long ____ to bake ____ it and I'll

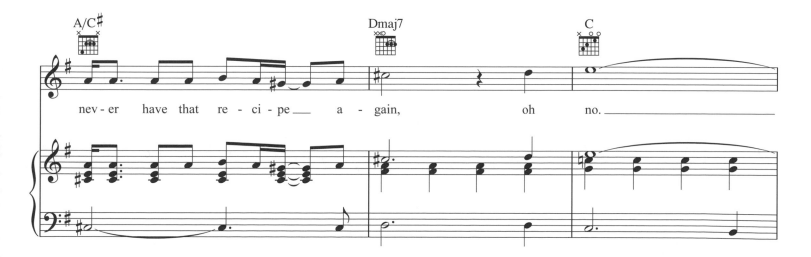

nev - er have that re - ci - pe ____ a - gain, oh no. _____

Uptempo Disco groove

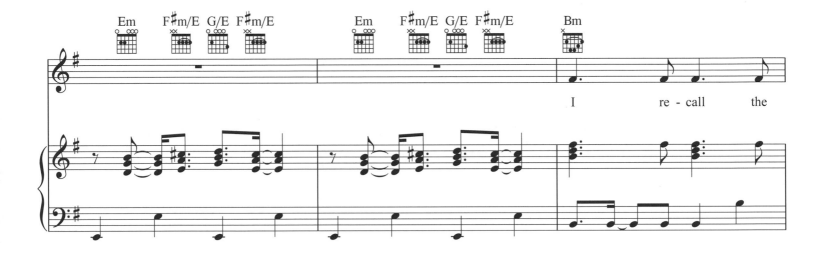

I re-call the

yel-low _____ cot-ton dress foam-ing like a wave _

on the ground be-neath your knees.

Birds like __ ten - der ba - bies in your

hands and the old men ___ play - ing ___ Chin - ese

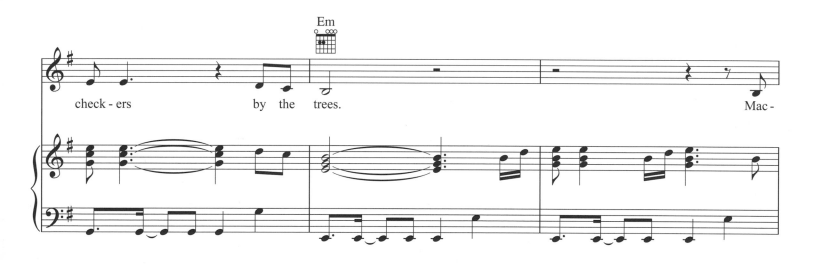

check - ers by the trees. Mac -

Ar - thur's Park __ is melt - ing in the dark, ___ all the

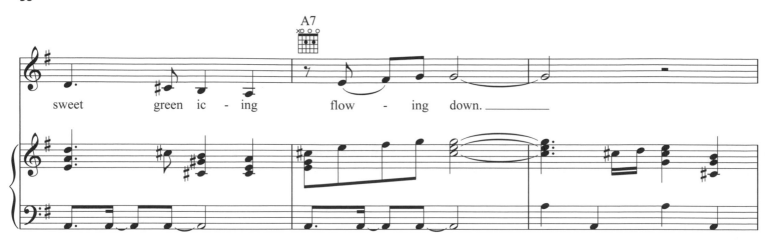

sweet green ic - ing flow - ing down. ____

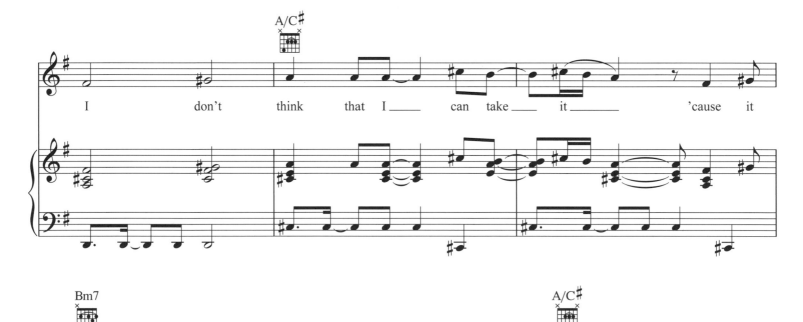

Some - one left the cake ____ out in the rain.

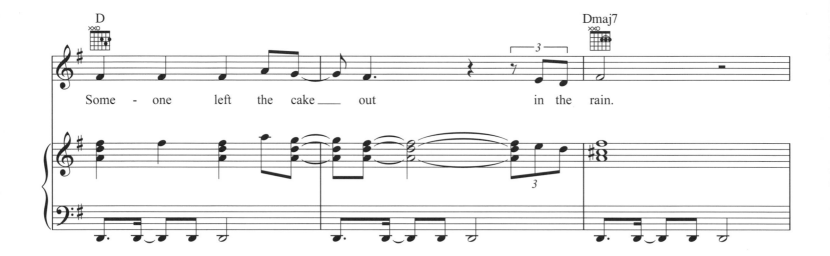

I don't think that I ____ can take ____ it ____ 'cause it

took so long ____ to bake ____ it and I'll nev - er have ____ that

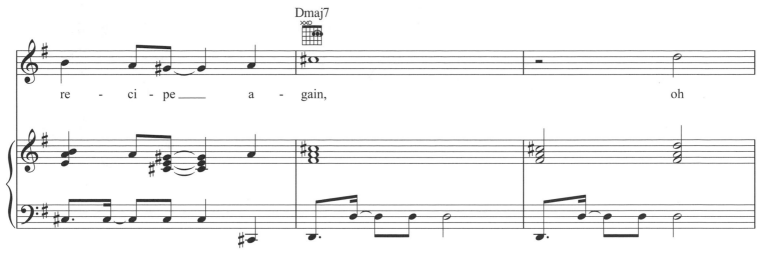

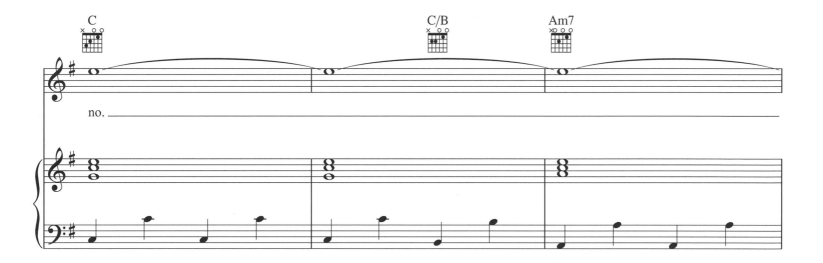

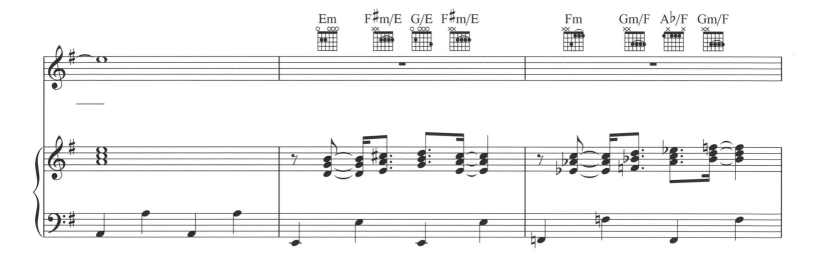

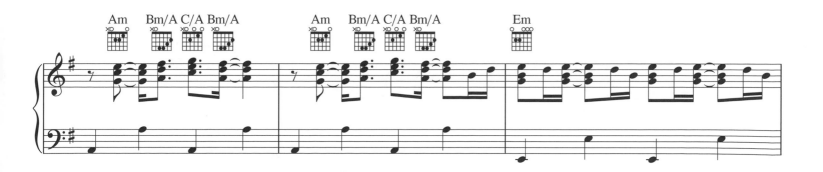

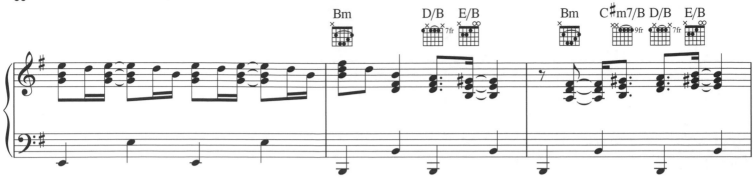

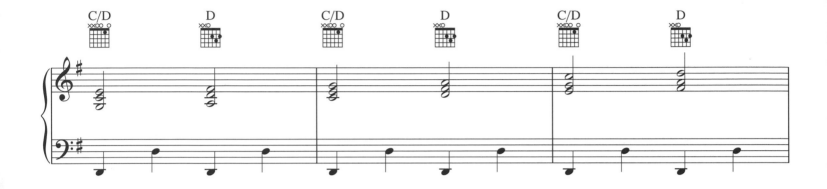

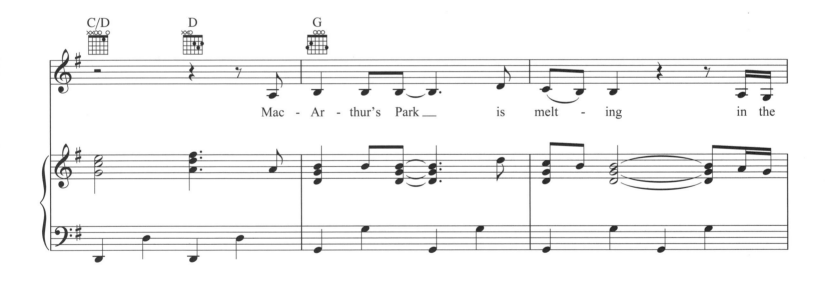

Mac - Ar - thur's Park __ is melt - ing in the

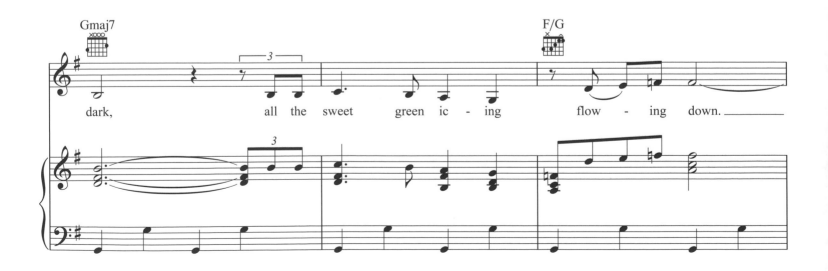

dark, all the sweet green ic - ing flow - ing down. ____

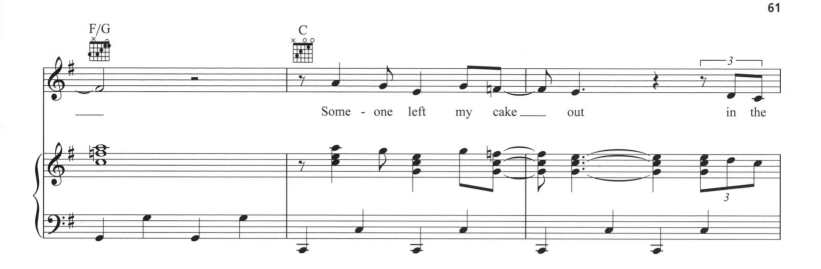

Some-one left my cake ___ out in the

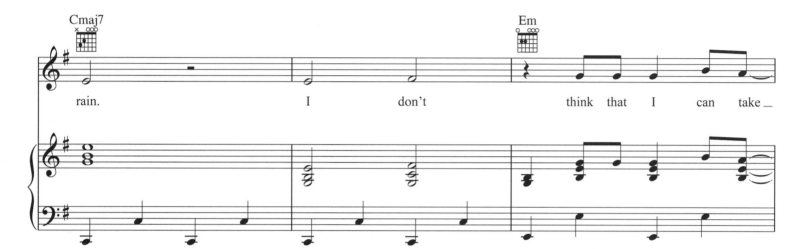

rain. I don't think that I can take ___

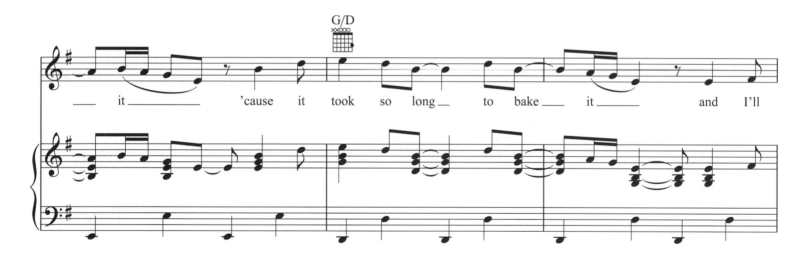

___ it ___ 'cause it took so long ___ to bake ___ it ___ and I'll

nev - er have ___ that re - ci - pe ___ a - gain,

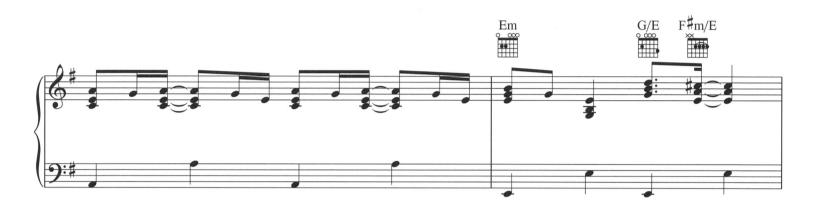

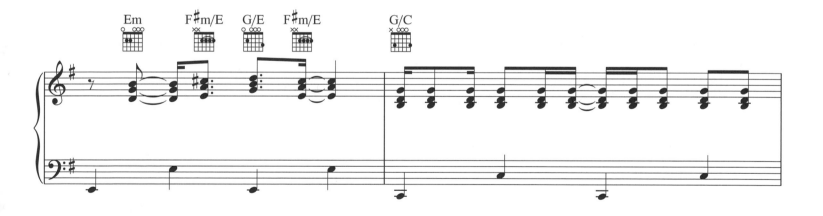

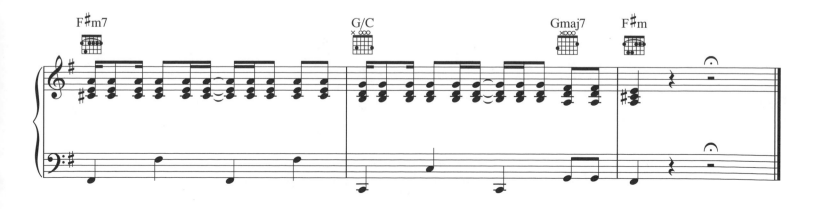

NO MORE TEARS
(Enough Is Enough)

Words and Music by PAUL JABARA
and BRUCE ROBERTS

It's rain-ing, it's pour-ing, my love life is bor-ing me to tears af-ter all these years. No sun-shine, no moon-light, no star-dust, no sign __ of ro-mance, we don't stand a chance.

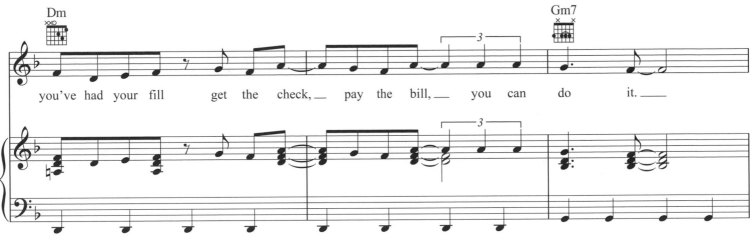

you've had your fill get the check,— pay the bill,— you can do it.—

Tell him to just — get out, — noth-

-ing left to talk — a-bout.— Pack his rain-coat,

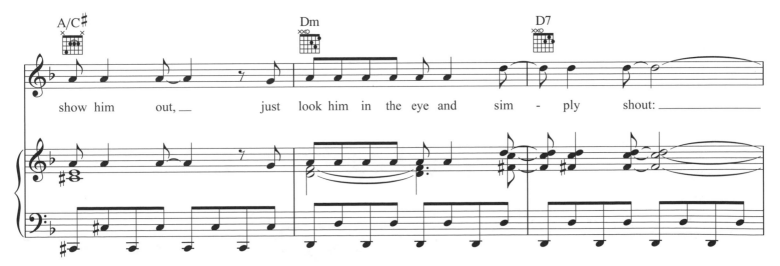

show him out,— just look him in the eye and sim-ply shout:_____

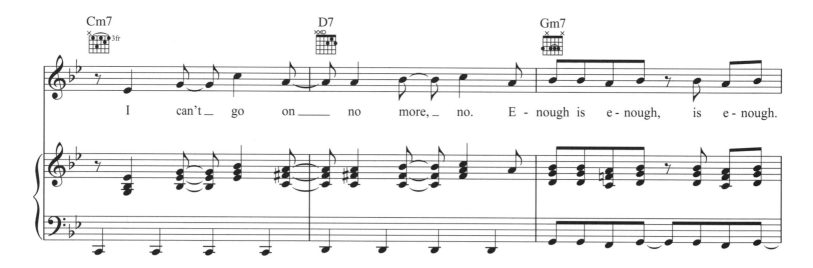

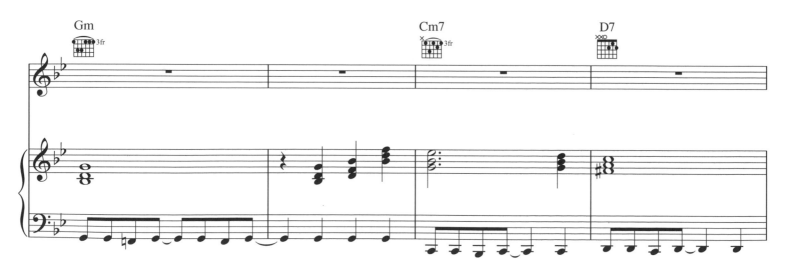

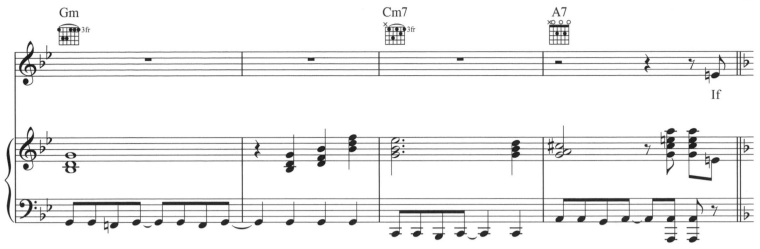

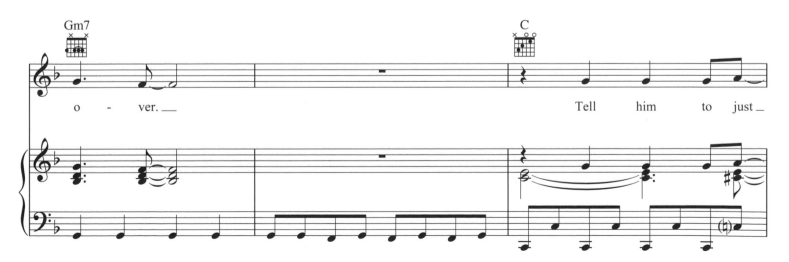

get out,___ say it clear-ly, spell it out.___

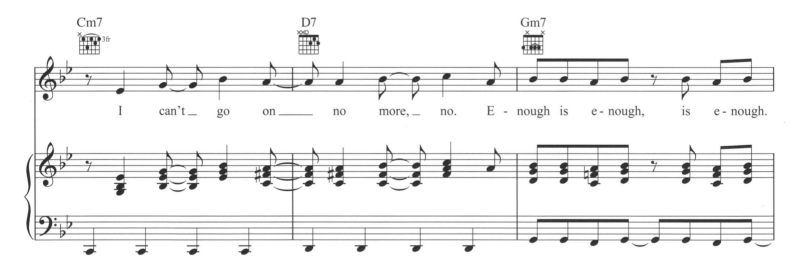

___ E - nough is e-nough, is e-nough. I can't__ go on,

I can't__ go on___ no more,__ no. E - nough is e-nough, is e-nough.

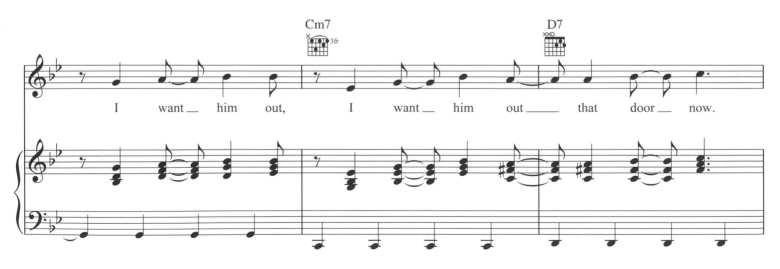

I want__ him out, I want__ him out___ that door__ now.

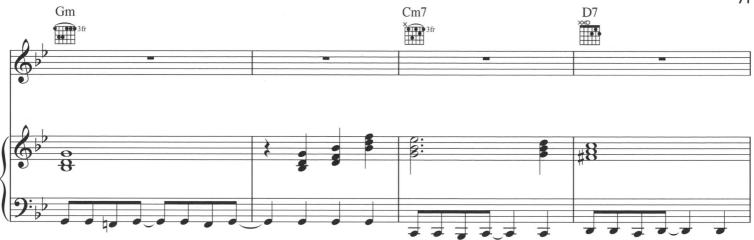

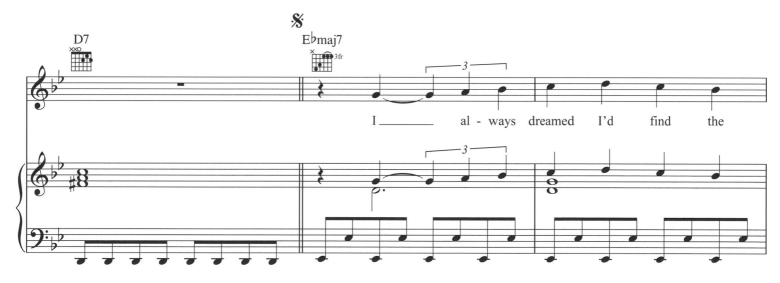

I _____ al - ways dreamed I'd find the

per - fect lov - er. ____ But he turned

out to be like ev - 'ry oth - er man I

loved, I had no choice _____ from the start. _____

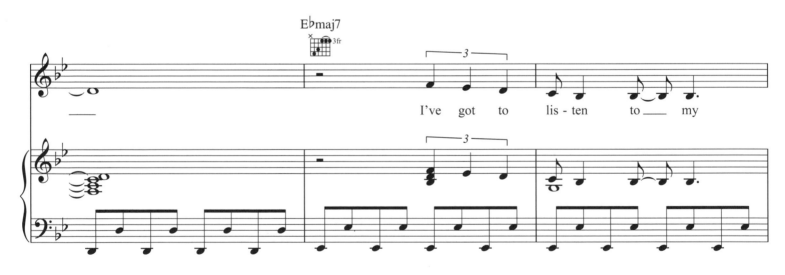

I've got to lis - ten to ___ my

heart tear - ing us a - part. _____

nough is e - nough, is e - nough. I can't_ go on, I can't_ go on _

_ no more,_ no. E - nough is e - nough, is e - nough. I want_ him out,

To Coda

I want _ him out _ that door _ now.

No more tears. ____

E - nough is e - nough is e - nough

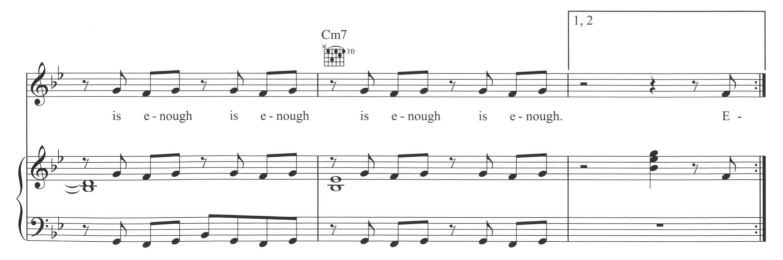

is e - nough is e - nough is e - nough is e - nough. E -

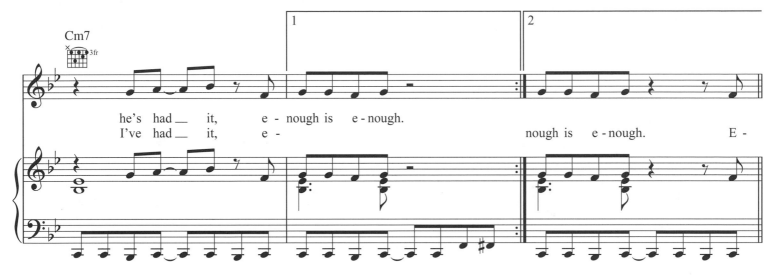

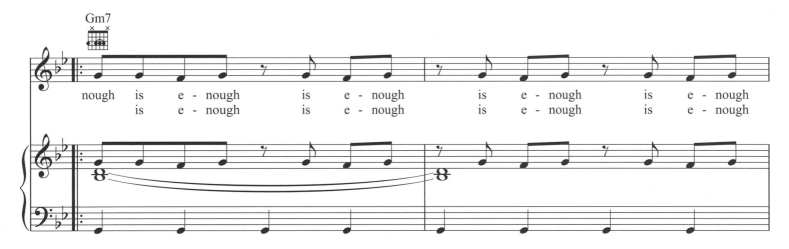

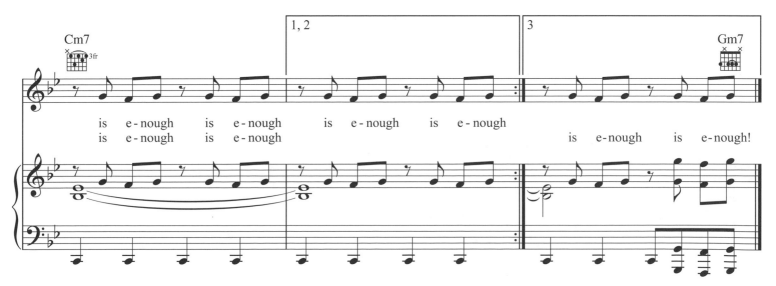

SHE WORKS HARD FOR THE MONEY

Words and Music by DONNA SUMMER
and MICHAEL OMARTIAN

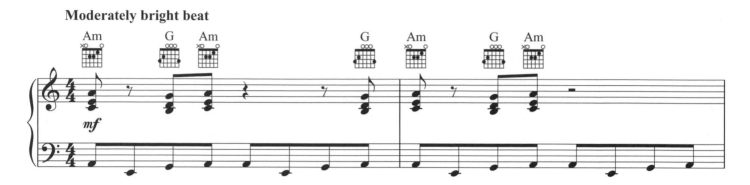

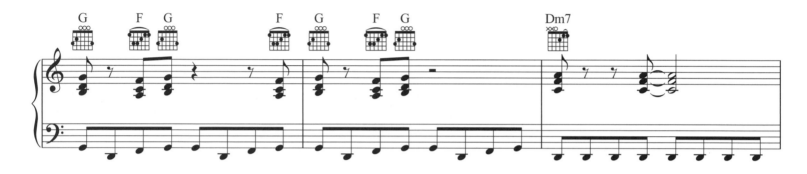

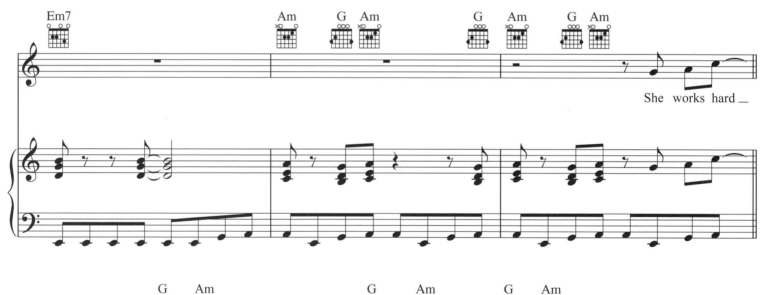

She works hard ___

___ for the mon - ey. So hard ___

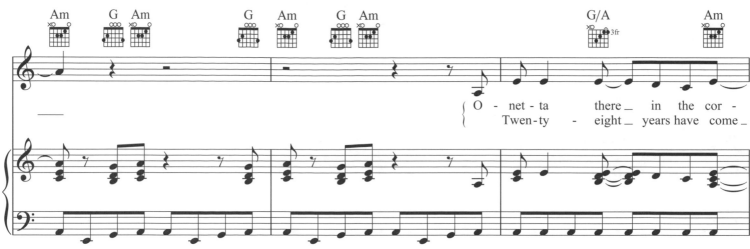

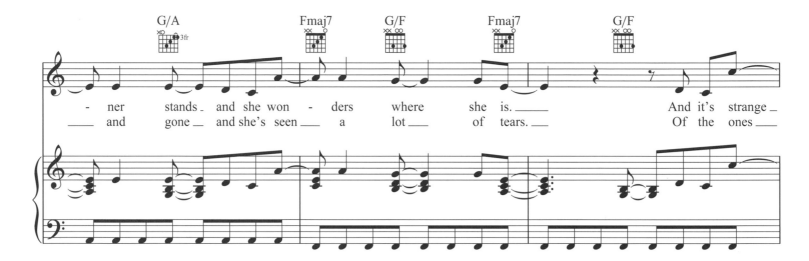

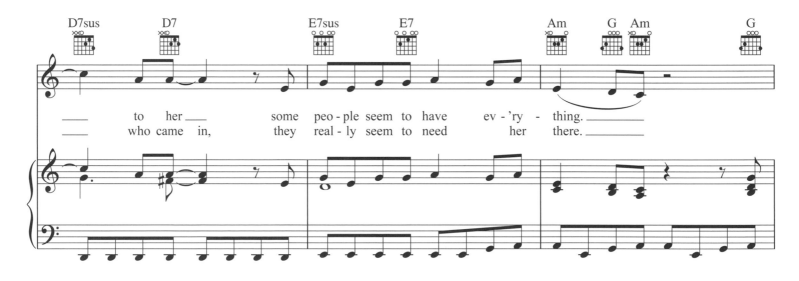

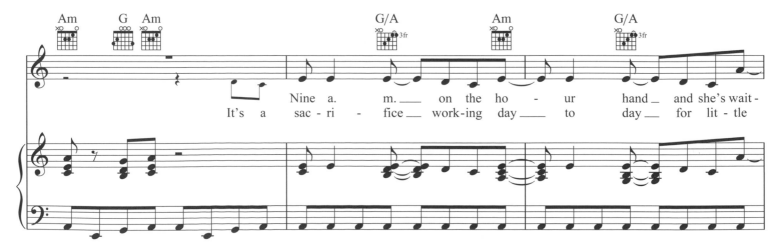

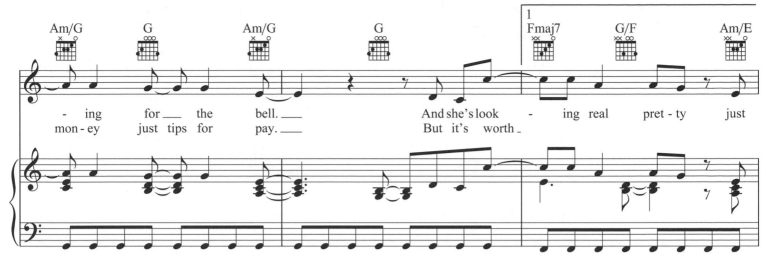

-ing for ___ the bell. ___ And she's look - ing real pret-ty just
mon - ey just tips for pay. ___ But it's worth

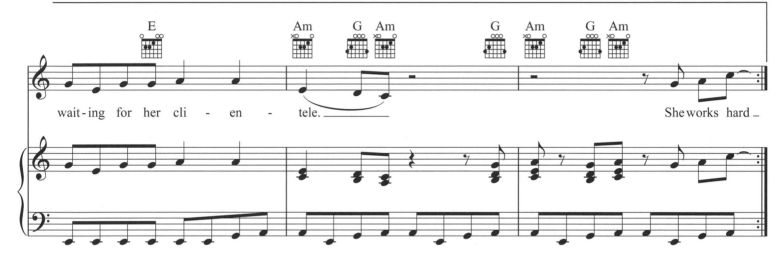

wait - ing for her cli - en - tele. ___ She works hard

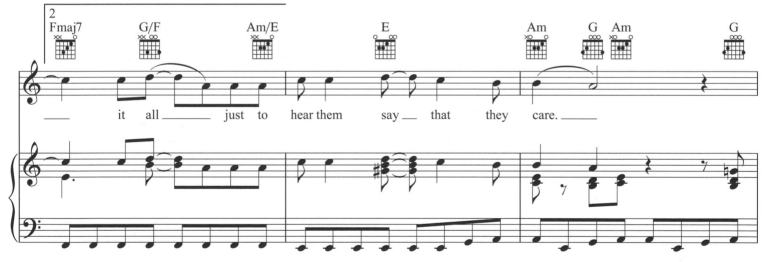

___ it all ___ just to hear them say ___ that they care. ___

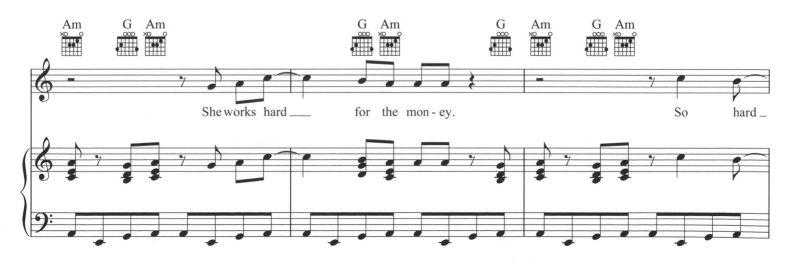

She works hard ___ for the mon - ey. So hard

for it, hon - ey.　　She works hard ___ for the mon - ey so you

bet - ter treat her right. ___

She al - read - y knows ___　　she's seen her bad ___

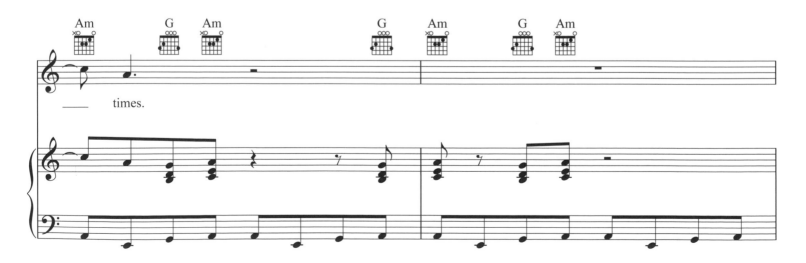

___ times.

STAMP YOUR FEET

Words and Music by DONNA SUMMER,
DANIELLE BRISEBOIS and GREGORY KURSTIN

Moderate Groove

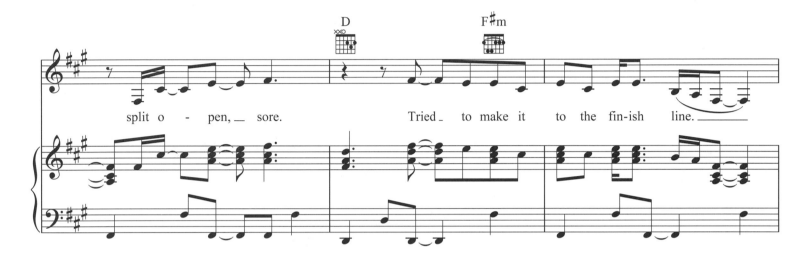

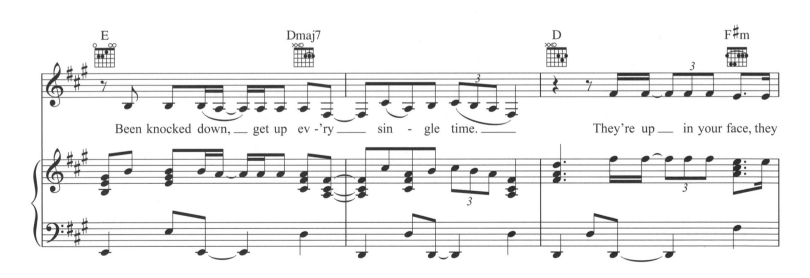

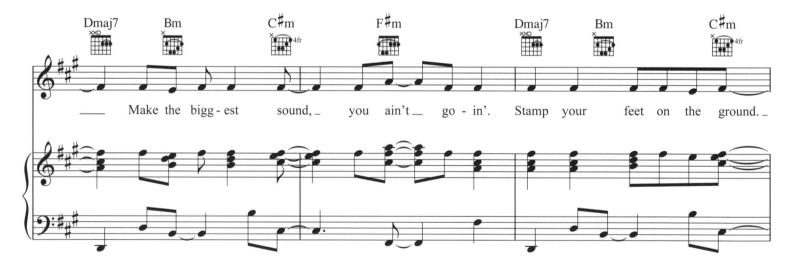

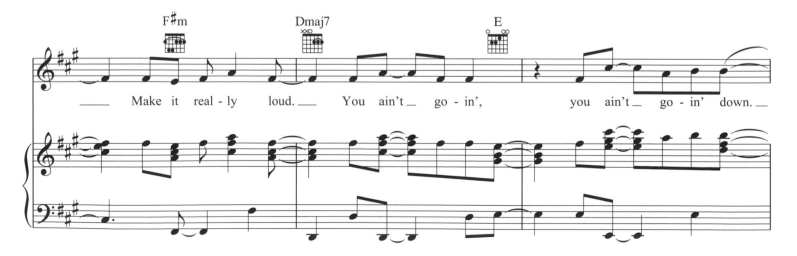

Rain __ comes in ev - 'ry play - ers life.

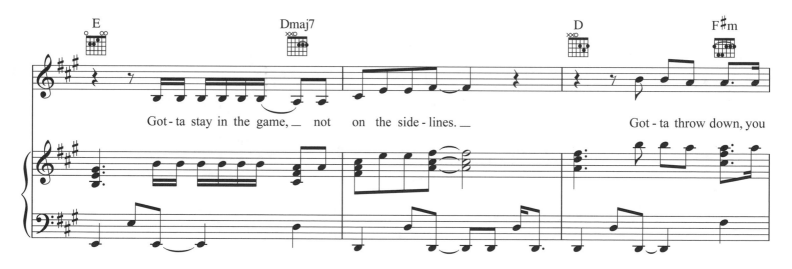

Got - ta stay in the game, __ not on the side - lines. __ Got - ta throw down, you

got - ta stand and fight. Keep your eye on the prize, don't get caught up in strife. __

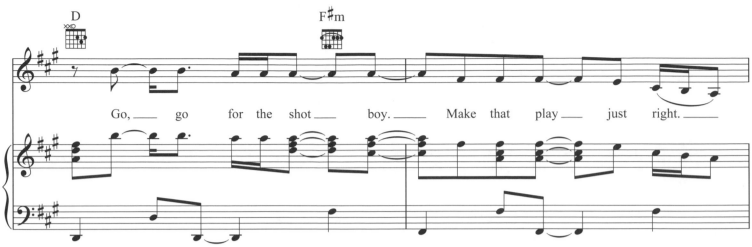

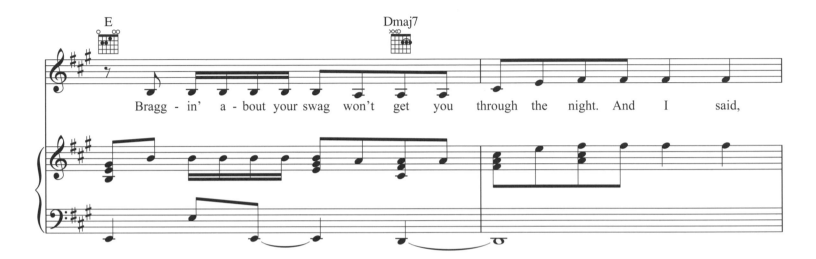

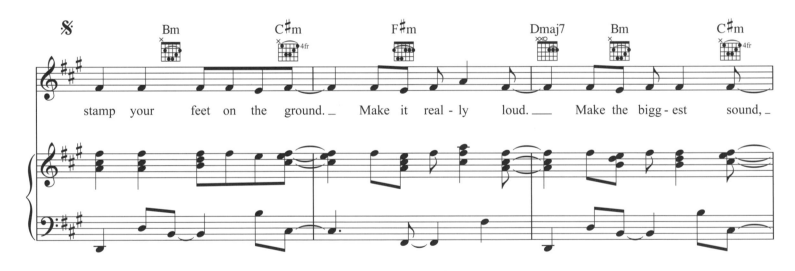

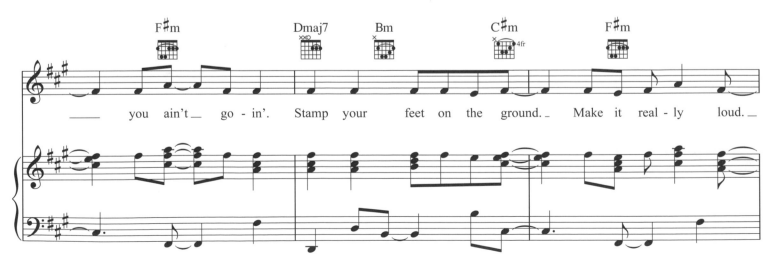

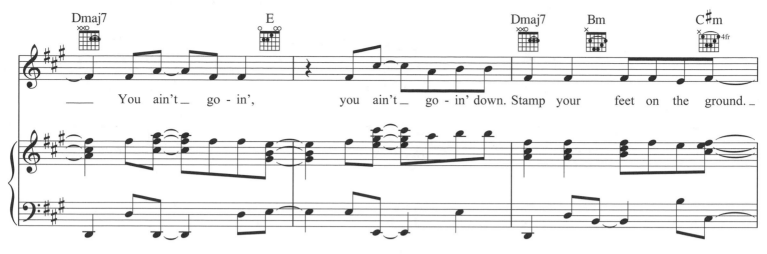

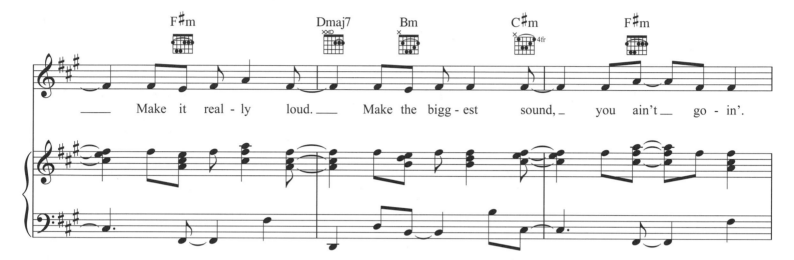

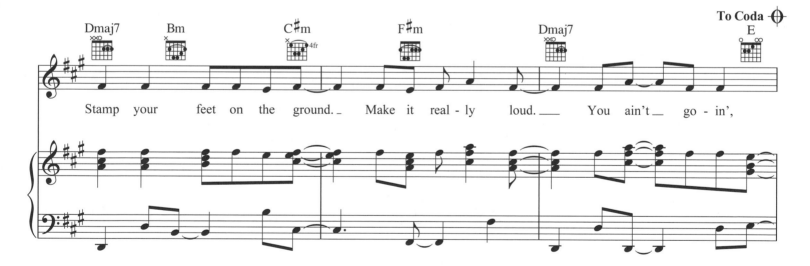

S - T - A - M - P, ___ stamp-in' on the ground. ___ S - T - A - M - P, ___
(You got fame.)

stamp-in' on the ground. ___ S - T - A - M - P, ___ We ain't_ go-in' down. ___
(You got a name.) *(Do that thang.)*

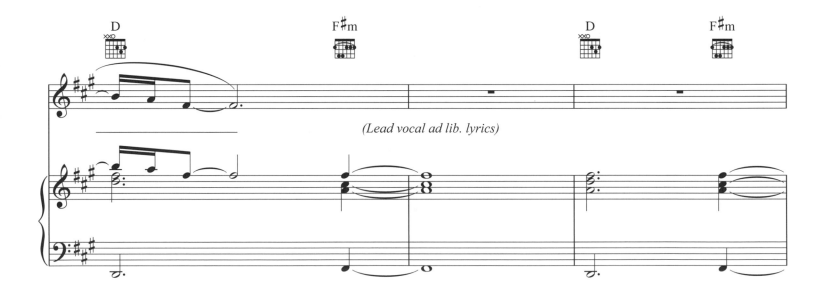

D   F#m   D   F#m

(Lead vocal ad lib. lyrics)

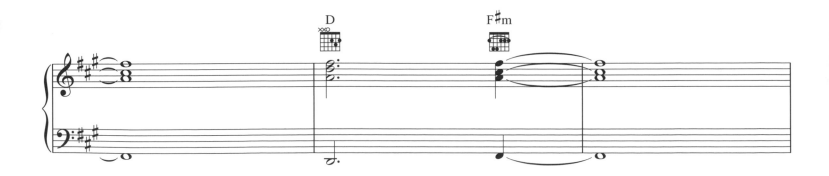

D   F#m

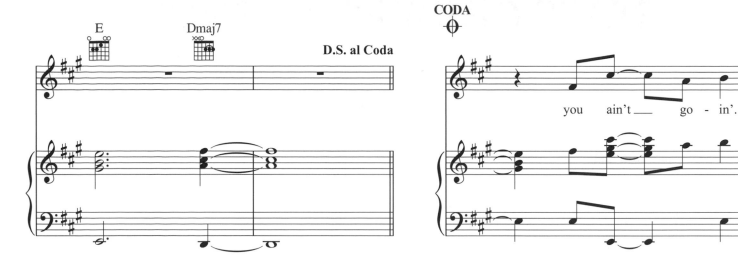

CODA

D.S. al Coda

you ain't___ go - in'.

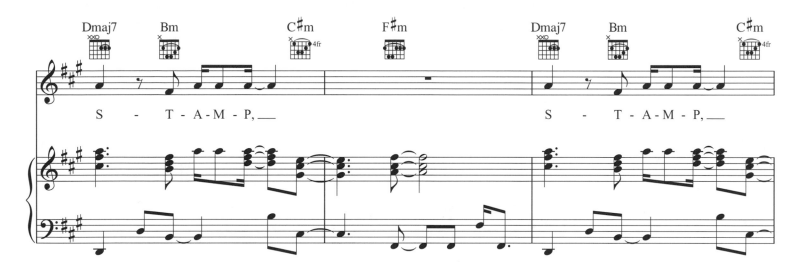

S - T - A - M - P,___ S - T - A - M - P,___

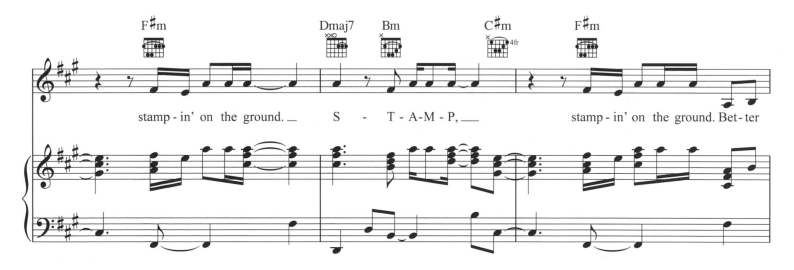

stamp - in' on the ground. ___ S - T - A - M - P,___ stamp - in' on the ground. Bet - ter

stamp your feet on the, stamp your feet on the ground. ___

STATE OF INDEPENDENCE

Words and Music by VANGELIS
and JON ANDERSON

Moderate Reggae

State of life,__ may I live, may I love. Com-ing out the sky, I made__ me a

* Recorded a half step higher.

name.

Com-ing out civ-il word for what it is. It is ___

___ the ver-y na-ture of ___ the sound, the game.

Sha-

bla-mi-di, sha-bla-mi-da, sha-bla-mi-di, sha-bla-mi-da, sha-bla-mi-di, sha-bla-mi-

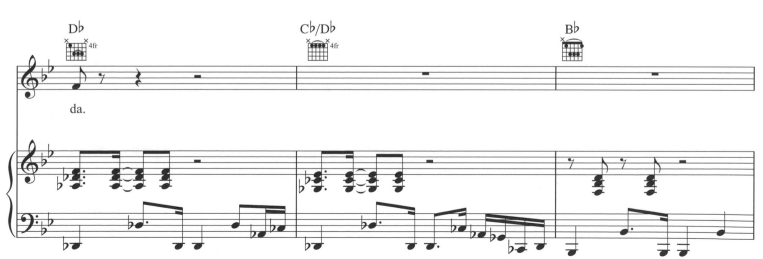

da.

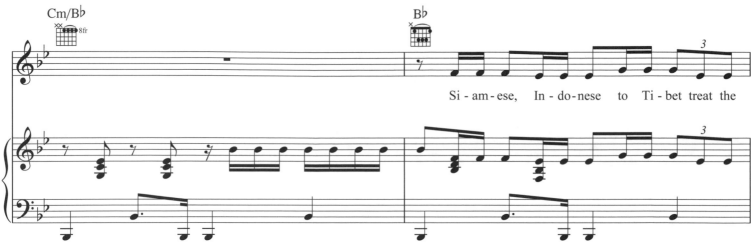

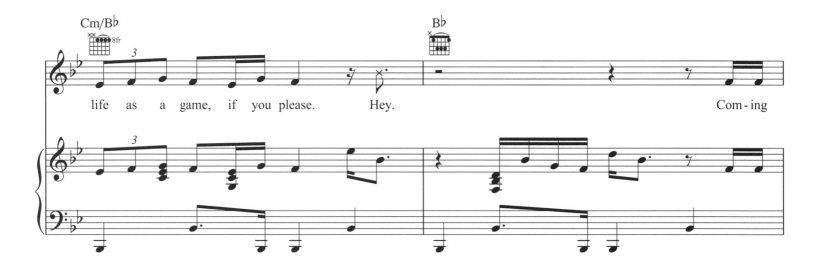

guessed __ it. Sha - bla - mi - di, sha - bla - mi - da, sha - bla - mi - di,

sha - bla - mi - da, sha - bla - mi - di, sha - bla - mi - da. Sha-

bla - mi - di, sha - bla - mi - da, sha - bla - mi - di, sha - bla - mi - da, sha - bla - mi - di, sha - bla - mi-

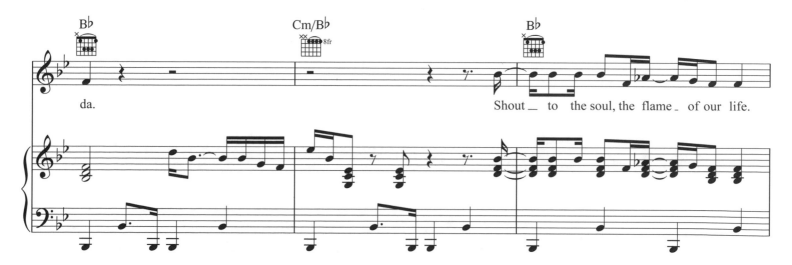

da. Shout __ to the soul, the flame __ of our life.

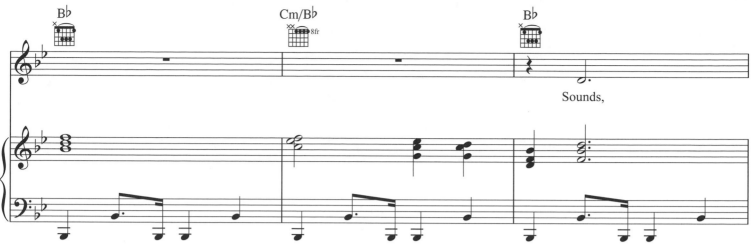

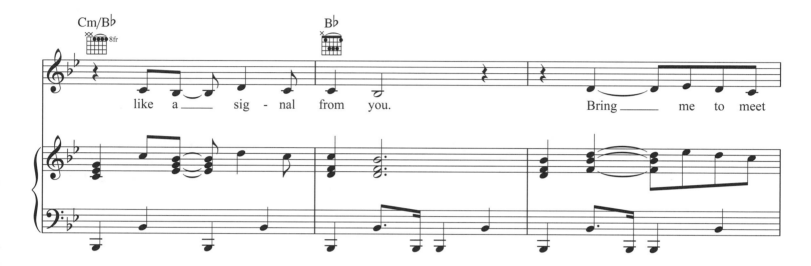

Touch - ing my __ bod - y, my __ soul. __ Bring to me, __

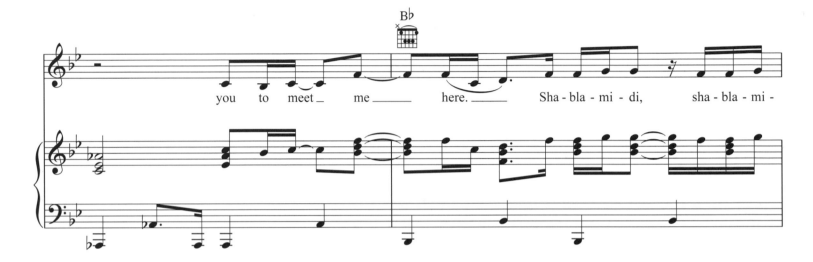

you to meet __ me __ here. __ Sha - bla - mi - di, sha - bla - mi -

da, sha - bla - mi - di, sha - bla - mi - da, Home,

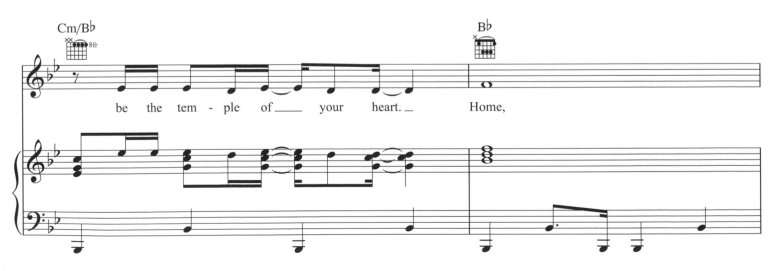

be the tem - ple of __ your heart. __ Home,

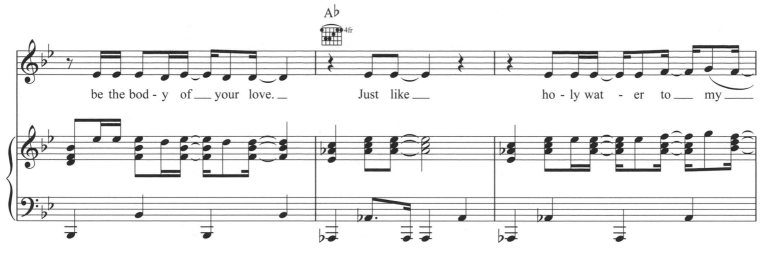

be the bod-y of ___ your love. ___ Just like ___ ho-ly wat-er to ___ my ___

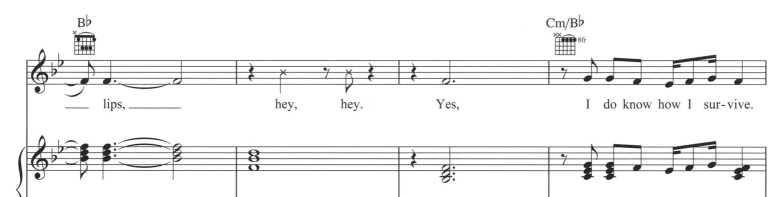

___ lips, _____ hey, hey. Yes, I do know how I sur-vive.

Yes, I do know why I'm a-live. To love and be with you ___

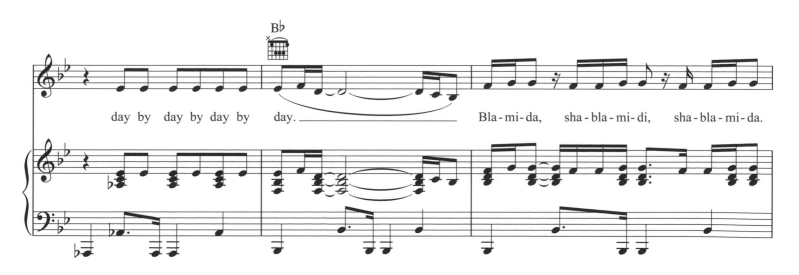

day by day by day by day. _____ Bla-mi-da, sha-bla-mi-di, sha-bla-mi-da.

THIS TIME I KNOW IT'S FOR REAL

Words and Music by DONNA SUMMER,
MATTHEW AITKEN, PETER WATERMAN
and MICHAEL STOCK

Moderate Dance groove

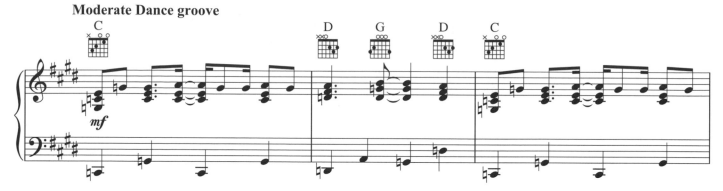

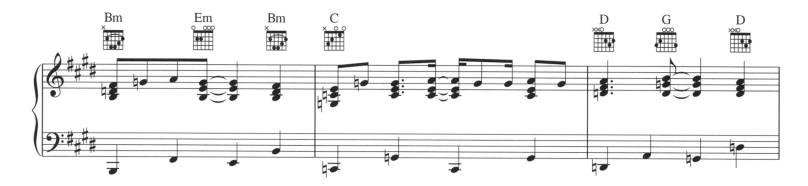

What would I have __ to do __
Should I write or call __ your home? __

E **A**

to get ____ you _____ to no - tice me too? _____ Do I ___
Shout it out ____ with a meg - a - phone. _____ Ra - di - o or

Am6 **E** **C#m**

stand _ in line, _____ one of the mill - ion ad - mir - ing eyes? _____
T - V news. ____ Got to find a way to get the mess - age to you. ___

Bm7 **Bm6** **A**

(1., D.S.) Walk a tight - rope way ___ up high. _____ Write your name a -
(2.) Say I love you with a ne - on sign. _____ An - y - thing to

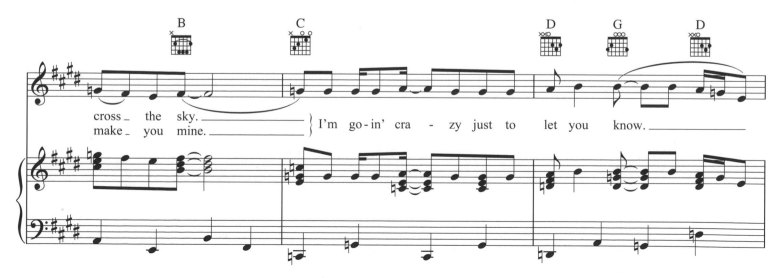

B **C** **D** **G** **D**

cross _ the sky. _____ } I'm go - in' cra - zy just to let you know. _____
make _ you mine. _____

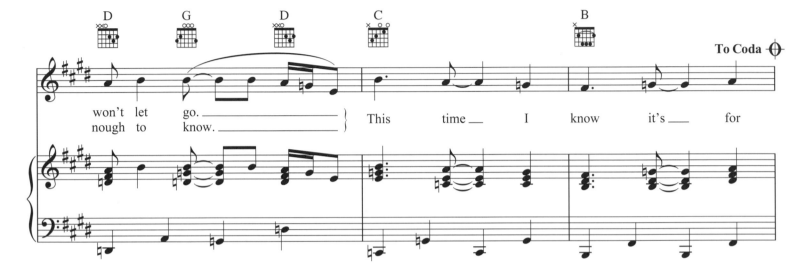

You'd be a- mazed_ how much I love you so,_____ ba-by. When I get my hands on you I
If I wait too long_ for you I might ex- plode, oh, ba-by. I've _been a- round the block e-

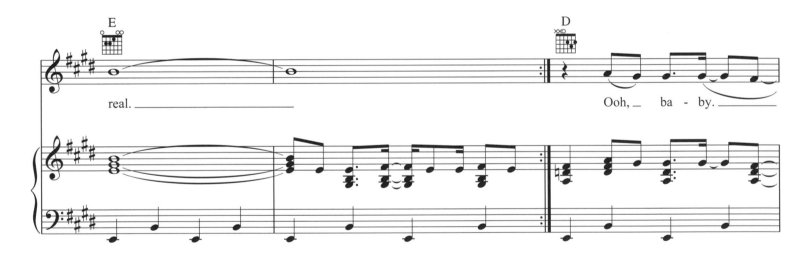

won't let go. _____ } This time _ I know it's _ for
nough to know. _____

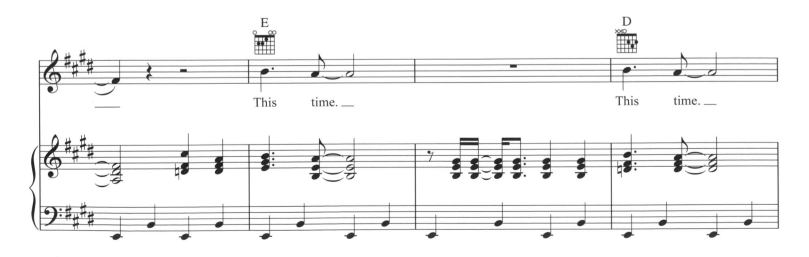

real. _____ Ooh, _ ba- by. _____

This time. _ This time. _

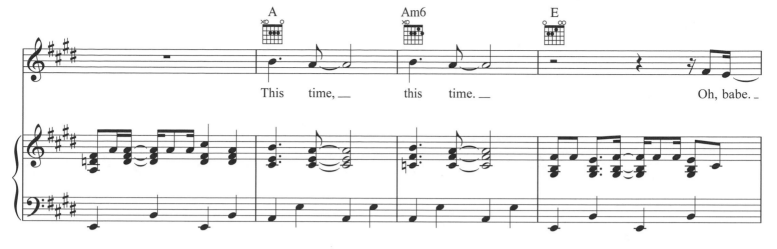

This time, __ this time. __ Oh, babe. __

__ This time, __ this time. __ Oh, babe.

D.S. al Coda

CODA

real. I'm go-in' cra - zy just to

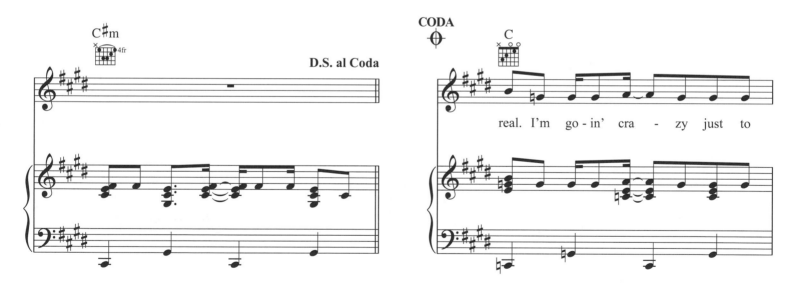

let you know. _____ If I wait too long _ for you I might ex - plode, _ oh, ba - by.

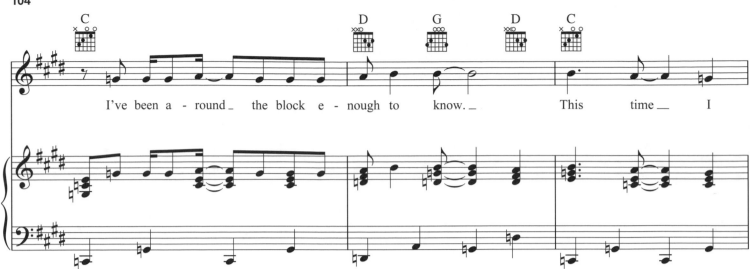

I've been a - round the block e - nough to know. This time I

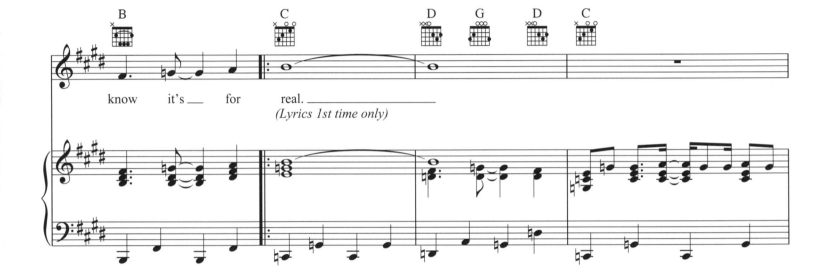

know it's for real.
(Lyrics 1st time only)

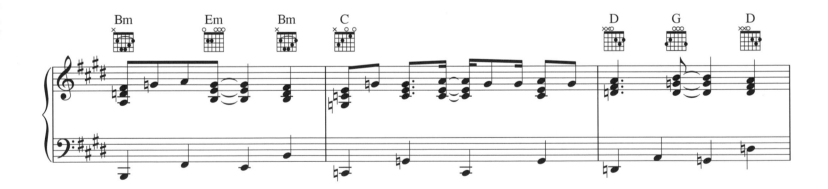

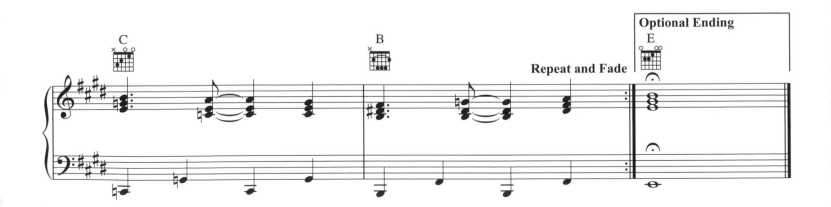

Optional Ending

Repeat and Fade

UNCONDITIONAL LOVE

Words and Music by DONNA SUMMER
and MICHAEL OMARTIAN

Moderate Calypso groove

What up man?
I want to say something to you.

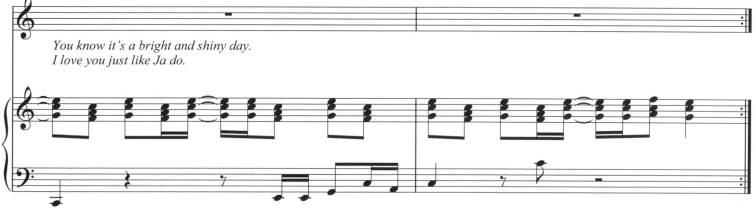

You know it's a bright and shiny day.
I love you just like Ja do.

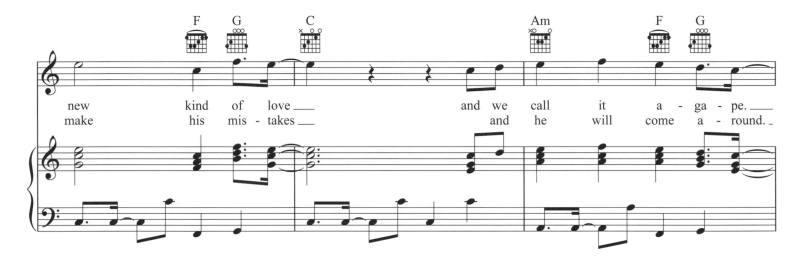

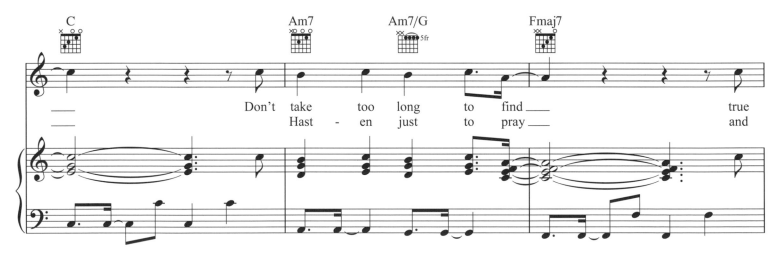

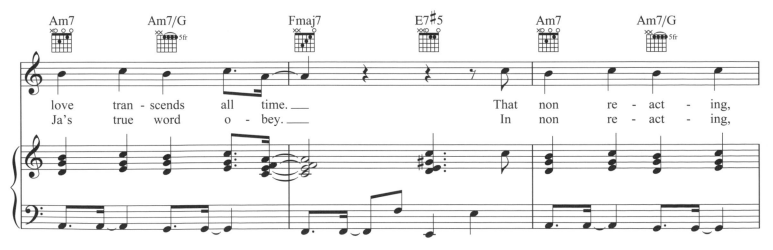

ev - er - last - ing love. _____
ev - er - last - ing love. _____
Give

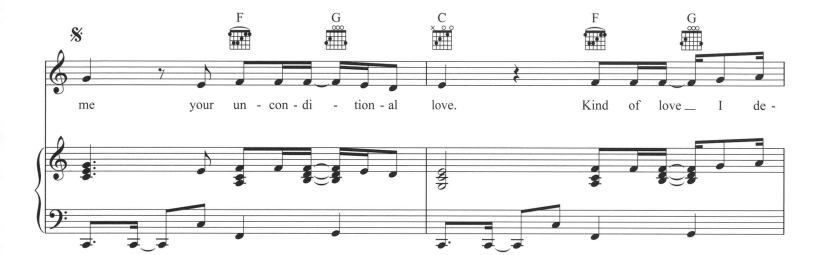

me your un - con - di - tion - al love. Kind of love _ I de -

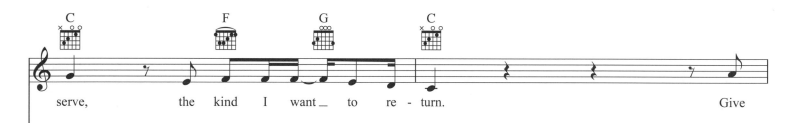

serve, the kind I want _ to re - turn. Give

me your un - con - di - tion - al love. Kind of love _ I de -

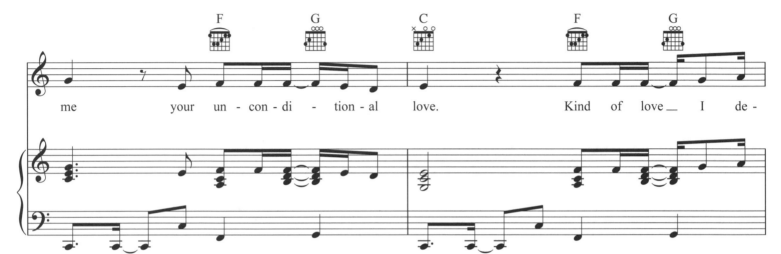

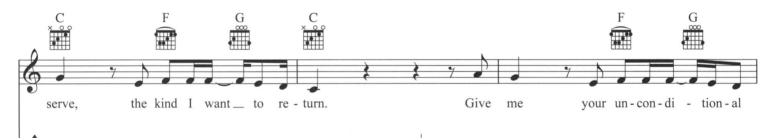

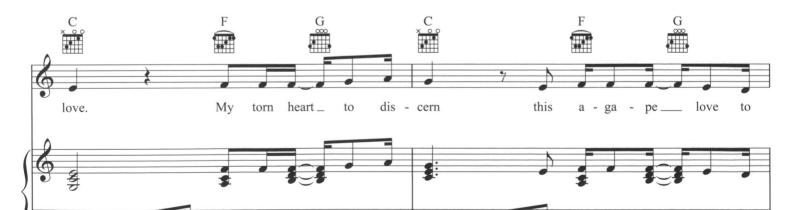

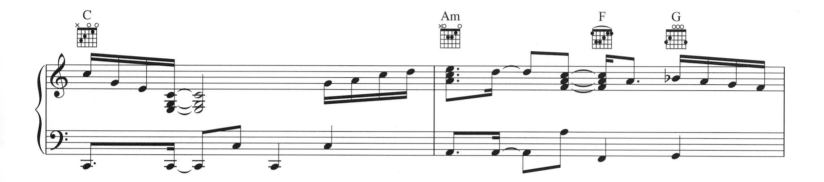

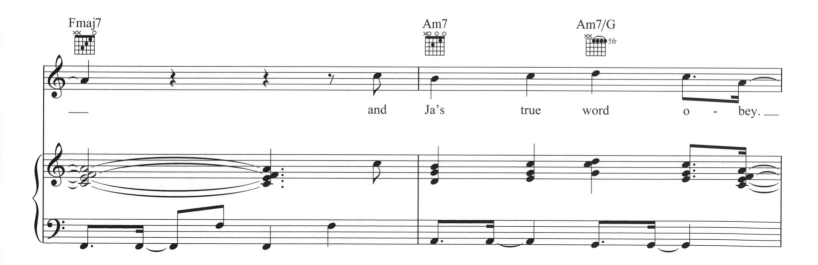

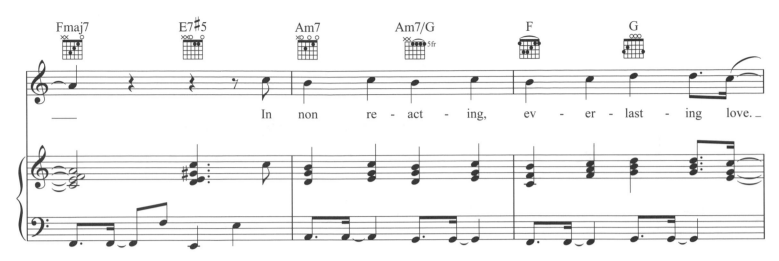

In non re - act - ing, ev - er - last - ing love.

D.S. al Coda

Give

CODA

turn. Give me your un - con - di - tion - al

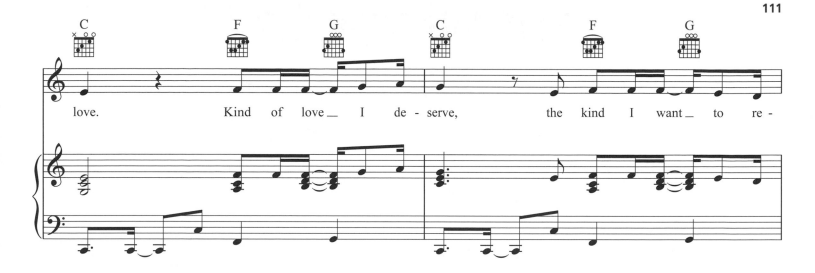

love. Kind of love __ I de - serve, the kind I want __ to re -

turn. Give me your un - con - di - tion - al

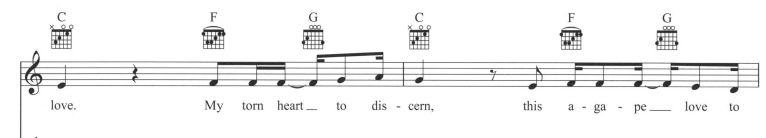

love. My torn heart __ to dis - cern, this a - ga - pe __ love to

Repeat and Fade

Optional Ending

learn. Give me your un - con - di - tion - al love.

THE WANDERER

Words and Music by DONNA SUMMER
and GIORGIO MORODER

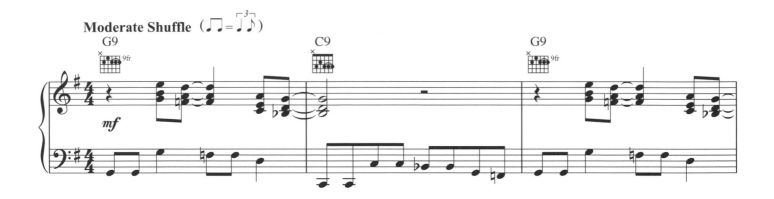

Woke up this morn-in', I dragged my - self a-cross the bed.
Slip down the back stair on my toes, then out the door.

I know I'm read-y now, it's just a lit-tle time. _ 'Cause I'm a wan-der-er. Ooh, _
No need to wor-ry 'cause I sel-dom am a-lone. _ 'Cause I'm a wan-der-er. Ooh, _
And I don't know if I could change your frame of mind. _ 'Cause I'm a wan-der-er. Ooh, _

____ I'm a wan-der-er. _
____ I'm a wan-der-er. _
just a wan-der-er. _

'Cause I'm a

wan-der-er, I trav-el ev-'ry place. _ 'Cause I'm a wan-der-er from here to

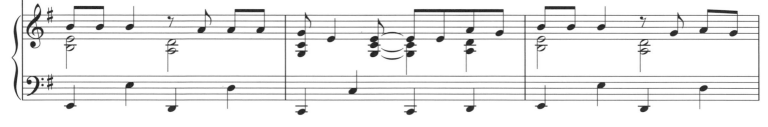

To Coda ⊕

out-er space. _ 'Cause I'm a wan-der-er, got no time. ____

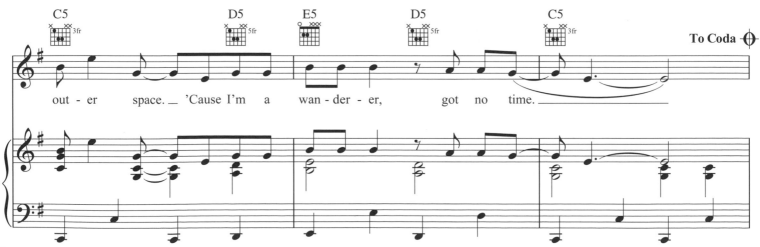

'Cause I'm a wan-der-er.   Ooh, ___   just a wan-der-er. ___

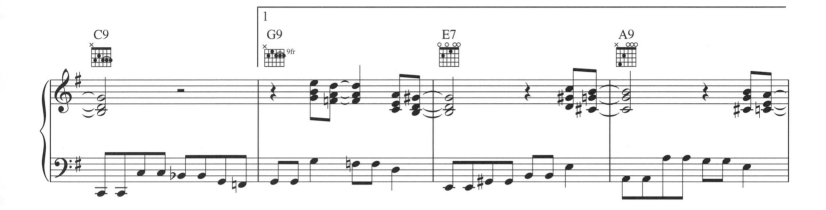

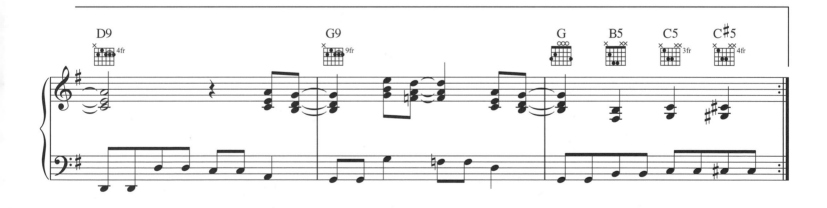

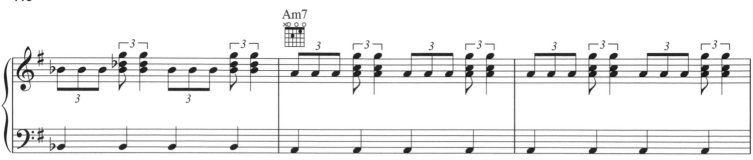

'Cause I'm a wan-

der - er. Ooh, ___ just a wan - der - er. ___

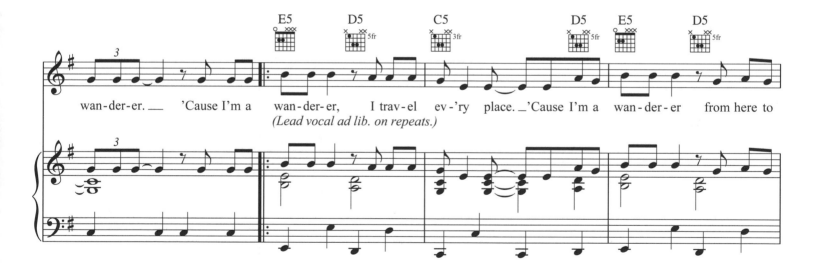